The Significance of the Temple Incident in the Narratives of the Four Gospels

The Significance of the Temple Incident in the Narratives of the Four Gospels

Deolito V. Vistar, Jr.

WIPF & STOCK · Eugene, Oregon

THE SIGNIFICANCE OF THE TEMPLE INCIDENT IN THE NARRATIVES OF THE FOUR GOSPELS

Copyright © 2018 Deolito V. Vistar, Jr. All rights reserved. Except for brief quotations in critical publications or reviews, no part of this book may be reproduced in any manner without prior written permission from the publisher. Write: Permissions, Wipf and Stock Publishers, 199 W. 8th Ave., Suite 3, Eugene, OR 97401.

Wipf & Stock
An Imprint of Wipf and Stock Publishers
199 W. 8th Ave., Suite 3
Eugene, OR 97401

www.wipfandstock.com

PAPERBACK ISBN: 978-1-5326-5477-0
HARDCOVER ISBN: 978-1-5326-5478-7
EBOOK ISBN: 978-1-5326-5479-4

Manufactured in the U.S.A.   10/16/18

Biblical quotations, unless otherwise noted, are from the New Revised Standard Version Bible, copyright © 1989, Division of Christian Education of the National Council of the Churches of Christ in the United States of America. Used by permission. All rights reserved.

*Affectionately dedicated to my wife, Guan Wang,
on the occasion of our seventh wedding anniversary*

Contents

Acknowledgments | ix
Abbreviations | x

1 Introduction | 1
2 The Significance of the Matthean Temple Incident | 7
3 The Significance of the Marcan Temple Incident | 30
4 The Significance of the Lucan Temple Incident | 64
5 The Significance of the Johannine Temple Incident | 84
6 Synthesis and Conclusions | 113

Appendix 1: Summative Comparison of the Four Gospels' Reports of the Temple Incident | 117
Appendix 2: Comparison of the Synoptic Gospels' Accounts of the Temple Incident | 119
Appendix 3: Comparison of Mark's and John's Accounts of the Temple Incident | 121

Bibliography | 125
Index of Subjects | 137
Index of Greek Words and Phrases | 139
Index of Authors | 141
Index of Ancient Documents | 145

Acknowledgments

THIS BOOK BEGAN LIFE during my graduate studies at Kosin University in Busan, South Korea, in the years 2012–2014. A huge thank you goes to the then–university president Dr. Sung-soo Kim, whose vision of an English-track graduate studies program in theology at Kosin University paved the way for the research of this book. Thanks are also due to Prof. Young-mog Song for supervising my research. A note of thanks also goes to the kind staff at the university's International Office, as well as to the helpful staff at the university's Theodore Hard Library.

During those years of my being away from home (in the Philippines), the Peniel Church and the Peniel International Christian Community in Busan became my home away from home. Special thanks go to the Rev. Do-myoung Kim (senior pastor) and Rev. Fisher Kim (then associate pastor). I also thank a few other local churches in Busan that embraced me as their own and where I was privileged to occasionally preach the Word: Baekyangro Church, Hosanna Church, and Shinpyeongro Church.

I thank my wife and best friend, Guan Wang, for her love and untiring support throughout the research and writing process. To her I lovingly dedicate this work. I also thank my mother, Debra, who never fails to pray for me.

Above all else, I thank the Almighty God—Father, Son, and Holy Spirit—for enabling me to write this book. I pray that this will bring honor to his name.

Deolito V. Vistar Jr.
Picton, New Zealand
July 2018

Abbreviations

ABD	*Anchor Bible Dictionary*, edited by David Noel Freedman, 6 vols. (New York: Doubleday, 1992)
A.J.	Josephus, *Antiquitates judaicae*
Ant.	Plutarch, *Antonius*
AUSS	*Andrews University Seminary Studies*
BBR	*Bulletin for Biblical Research*
BDAG	Walter Bauer, Frederick W. Danker, W. F. Arndt, and F. W. Gingrich, *Greek-English Lexicon of the New Testament and Other Early Christian Literature*, 3rd ed. (Chicago: University of Chicago Press, 2000)
BDF	Friedrich Blass and Albert Debrunner, translated and revised by Robert W. Funk, *A Greek Grammar of the New Testament and Other Early Christian Literature* (Chicago: University of Chicago Press, 1961)
Bek.	Bekorot
BEvT	Beiträge zur evangelischen Theologie
Bib	*Biblica*
BibInt	*Biblical Interpretation*
BibSac	*Bibliotheca Sacra*
B.J.	Josephus, *Bellum judaicum*
BJRL	*Bulletin of the John Rylands University Library of Manchester*
BR	*Biblical Research*
BT	*The Bible Translator*
BTB	*Biblical Theology Bulletin*

C. Ap.	Josephus, *Contra Apionem*
CBQ	*Catholic Biblical Quarterly*
CD	Cairo Genizah copy of the Damascus Document
Comm. Matt.	Origen, *Commentarii in evangelium Matthaei*
CTR	*Criswell Theological Review*
Dial.	Justin, *Dialogue with Trypho*
Directions	*Directions*
EBC	*Expositor's Bible Commentary*, edited by Frank E. Gaebelein, 12 vols. (Grand Rapids: Zondervan, 1976–1992)
ExpTim	*Expository Times*
FM	*Faith and Mission*
GELS	*A Greek-English Lexicon of the Septuagint*, by Takamitsu Muraoka (Leuven: Peeters, 2009)
Haer.	Irenaeus, *Against Heresies*
Hist. eccl.	Eusebius, *Historia ecclesiastica*
Hyp.	Clement of Alexandria, *Hypotyposes*
Int	*Interpretation*
JBL	*Journal of Biblical Literature*
JETS	*Journal of the Evangelical Theological Society*
JSNT	*Journal for the Study of the New Testament*
KENTS	*Korean Evangelical New Testament Studies*
Ker.	Keritot
Ketub.	Ketubbot
LCL	Loeb Classical Library
L&S	*Letter & Spirit*
LSJ	Henry George Liddell, Robert Scott, and Henry Stuart Jones, *A Greek-English Lexicon*, 9th ed. (Oxford: Clarendon, 1996)
Marc.	Tertullian, *Against Marcion*
NIB	*The New Interpreter's Bible*, edited by Leander E. Keck, 12 vols. (Nashville: Abingdon, 1994–2004)
NPNF²	*Nicene and Post-Nicene Fathers*, Series 2
NOAB	*New Oxford Annotated Bible*, 4th ed. (Oxford: Oxford University Press, 2010)

Abbreviations

NovT	*Novum Testamentum*
NTS	*New Testament Studies*
PRSt	*Perspectives in Religious Studies*
1QM	*Milḥamah* or *War Scroll*
1QS	*Serek Hayaḥad* or *Rule of the Community*
RevExp	*Review and Expositor*
Sir	Sirach
Spec. Laws	Philo, *On the Special Laws*
TDNT	*Theological Dictionary of the New Testament*, edited by Gerhard Kittel and Gerhard Friedrich, translated by Geoffrey W. Bromiley, 10 vols. (Grand Rapids: Eerdmans, 1964–76)
TJ	*Trinity Journal*
T. Mos.	*Testament of Moses*
VE	*Vox evangelica*

1

Introduction

INTRODUCTORY REMARKS

JESUS' PROTEST IN THE temple, referred to here simply as the temple incident,[1] recorded by all four evangelists,[2] can provide much insight for our understanding of Jesus, Judaism, and the relations between the two. It is perhaps for this reason that a host of interpreters have engaged this pericope for a very long time now with varying results.[3] Treatments of this subject have appeared in monographs and journals, and many commentaries have unsurprisingly also taken it up at length.[4]

Two observations can be made about most of these scholarly efforts. First, scholars have focused their attention mainly on the question of the probable motivation of the historical Jesus for his actions. Why did Jesus protest in the temple precincts? What was he protesting against? This focus has resulted in several varying, and often conflicting, proposals and

---

1. At times in this book I will also use the traditional expression temple "cleansing," without presupposing the attendant view that Jesus' motive for his act was to cleanse the temple.

2. Matt 21:12-13; Mark 11:15-19; Luke 19:45-46; John 2:13-22.

3. For a useful overview see Richardson, "Why Turn the Tables?"; Collins, "Jesus' Action."

4. E.g., Brown, *Gospel*, 1:112-25; Carson, *Gospel*, 175-84; Gundry, *Mark*, 639-47; Hagner, *Matthew 1-13*, 597-603; Bock, *Luke 9:51—24:53*, 1571-81; Davies and Allison, *Matthew*, 3:132-46; Keener, *Gospel*, 1:517-31; France, *Gospel*, 782-90.

conclusions. What seems clear, however, is that, insofar as the records of the evangelists are concerned, Jesus seemed to have had multiple purposes or motivations (though not of equal importance).[5] So it seems that scholarly preoccupation on the probable motivation of the historical Jesus has had its run, and that it is time for a shift of focus.

Second, one such area that has not yet been sufficiently investigated is the narratival meaning or significance that the temple incident plays in the Gospels. Put differently, what significance has each evangelist sought to invest into the temple incident as he composed his respective Gospel? I am here using the word "significance" to mean *meaning*. Hence in this study the question "What is the significance of the temple incident according to John?" is equivalent to the question of the meaning of the incident within the narrative of John's Gospel. The reason for this decision is apparent: "meaning" is itself a very fluid, ambiguous, and confusing word. So it is helpful here to define it by the word "significance" and to locate that within the whole of a given narrative itself.

It is now a general consensus that the evangelists were historians and theologians alike.[6] Long gone is the assumption that the evangelists were disinteresred "copy-paste" editors or collectors of first-century traditions. The evangelists composed their respective Gospel accounts with predetermined goals and emphases, which are accessible to us via the Gospel texts.

AIM AND OBJECTIVES

The aim of this study is to contribute to a better understanding of the significance of the temple incident in each of the canonical Gospels. To achieve this, the following objectives will be pursued.

First, we will identify, state, and analyze the immediate and broader contexts of each Gospel. By broader contexts I mean the big picture of the Gospels, and in pursuit of that we need to touch on issues of probable authorship, dating, recipients, occasion of writing, purposes, emphases, and outline. Immediate contexts pertain to what immediately surrounds the temple incident pericope. For example, in the case of the Mattean temple incident (21:12–13), the immediate contexts include Jesus' entry into Jerusalem (21:1–11) and his acts of healing in the temple (21:14–17).

---

5. The following chapters seek to demonstrate this.

6. See, for example, Marshall's discussion of history and theology in ch. 2 of his *Luke: Historian and Theologian*.

Second, we will analyze the language and thought of the subject-pericope and express its main idea. Third, we will try to establish the connections of the main idea to the overall message and main emphasis of each Gospel. Finally, we will enunciate the meaning of the temple incident in the light of all of the above.

CENTRAL ARGUMENT

The central theoretical argument of this book is that the significance of the temple incident is established by each evangelist according to his literary and theological purposes. Therefore, its significance ("meaning") varies from one evangelist to another.

The significance of the temple incident in Matthew is that it assists the readers to see Jesus as the prophesied Davidic Messiah who has authority over and concern for the temple. Jesus expresses that authority and concern not by cursing the temple but by clearing it of sellers and buyers, allowing the blind and the lame into the temple and healing them there, and receiving acclaim from children gathered in the temple precincts who acclaim him as the Son of David.

The significance of the temple incident in Mark is that it symbolizes God's sovereign and righteous judgment upon the temple for its apparent failure to produce fruits that God had desired. Jesus' actions—driving out the sellers and buyers and the animals, overturning tables and chairs, and blockading the passage of goods—must be seen not as acts of cleansing but as symbolic of the dissolution of the temple as a result of God's judgment.

The significance of the incident in Luke lies in its balancing two realities about the temple: that it is under God's rightful judgment and that, nevertheless, it still serves as a venue for Jesus' ministry of teaching and healing.

Finally, the significance of the incident in John lies in what it affirms about John's view of Jesus as not only the ultimate sacrifice for the salvation of the world, but also as the new temple superseding the temple in Jerusalem.

PRESUPPOSITIONS AND METHODOLOGY

The main methodology employed in this study is a variation of composition criticism. According to Randall Tan, composition criticism is a kind of redaction criticism that "locates the patterns and emphases of the evangelists without systematically identifying or separating out redaction from tradition," in contrast to another kind of redaction criticism that "looks for the evangelists' theology in the redactional text after separating out redaction from tradition by means of source and form criticism."[7] Some works that have employed composition criticism are O'Toole's study of Luke (1984) and Kingsbury's study of Matthew (1975). More recent works include Willits (2007) and Hood (2011).

Specifically, composition criticism employed in this study will be characterized by the following. First, a focus on the work itself, that is, on the final text rather on the putative sources. The working presupposition is that "the work itself, viewed vigorously and persistently in its entirety, becomes the primary context for interpreting any part of it."[8] Second, a focus on the work's backgrounds. These include matters of authorship, purposes, recipients, the recipients' probable life settings (*Sitz im Leben*), and related issues. The working presupposition is that the Gospels are historical documents and must be understood in the light of the author's and readers' historical backgrounds. Thirdly, a focus on the author's theology. The working presupposition is that the evangelists wrote out accounts of Jesus' life and work from their theological vantage points and for their own theological purposes.

CHAPTER DIVISION

Chapter 1: Introduction

This chapter lays out the theoretical framework for this book: the statement of the problem, the aim and objectives, the central theoretical argument, and the research presuppositions and methodology.

Chapter 2: The Significance of the Matthean Temple Incident

This chapter proceeds in three interrelated movements or steps. The first seeks to grasp the big picture of Matthew's Gospel. What is this Gospel about? Who wrote it? When? Who were its recipients? Why was it written? What was the probable life setting of its intended readers? What are

---

7. Tan, "Developments," 600.
8. Moore, *Criticism*, 4.

its themes and emphases? The second movement focuses on the immediate contexts of the Matthean temple incident, namely Jesus' entrance into Jerusalem (21:1–11) and the healing, acclamation, and controversy in the temple (21:14–17). Part of the second movement is an analysis of the temple incident itself. We will analyze its language, determine its structure, and identify its key themes and emphases. Then, in the third and final movement, we step back and inquire how the themes and emphases of the subject-pericope cohere with Matthew's overall message, emphases, and purposes. At this point we will be able to articulate the meaning or significance of the temple incident according to Matthew.

Chapter 3: The Significance of the Marcan Temple Incident

As does chapter 2, this chapter will proceed in three movements. We will first seek to grasp the big picture of Mark's Gospel. What is this book about? Who wrote it? When? Who were its intended recipients? Why was it written? What was the probable life setting of its intended readers? What are its themes and emphases? Secondly, we will focus on the immediate contexts of the Markan temple incident, namely Jesus' entry into Jerusalem (11:1–11) and the cursing of the fig tree (11:12–14, 20–26). We will then analyze the Markan temple incident pericope (11:15–19)—its language, structure, and themes and emphases. In the final movement we will step back and inquire how the overall message and key themes and emphases of the pericope cohere with Mark's overall message, emphases, and purposes. We will then be able to articulate Mark's distinctive meaning for the temple incident.

Chapter 4: The Significance of the Lucan Temple Incident

The same procedure as in chapters 2 and 3 will be followed here. We will first try to grasp the big picture of Luke's Gospel. The same questions raised above will be investigated. In the second step, we will consider the immediate contexts of the Lukan temple incident, namely Jesus entry into Jerusalem (19:28–40), his lament over Jerusalem (19:41–44), and his daily teaching in the temple (19:47–48). We will then study the temple incident itself (19:45–46), understanding its language, determining its structure, and identifying its themes and emphases. Then in the final movement we will take a step back and ask how these themes and emphases cohere with the overall message and emphases of Luke's Gospel. We will then be able to articulate the Lukan distinctive significance for the temple incident.

Chapter 5: The Significance of the Johannine Temple Incident

Following the same procedure as in the above, we will first attempt to grasp the big picture of John's Gospel by answering the same questions as cited above. Second, we will analyze the immediate contexts of the Johannine temple incident, namely the first miracle in Cana (2:1–11) and the summative statement of unbelief in Jerusalem (2:23–25). Then we will analyze the Johannine temple incident itself, identifying its message, key themes, and emphases. Thirdly, we will figure out how these fit within the overall message of John's Gospel. Thereafter we will be able to articulate the distinctive Johannine perspective on the actions of Jesus in the temple.

Chapter 6: Synthesis and Conclusions

This chapter concludes this study with a table containing a summative synthesis and conclusions. There is also a recommendaiton for further research.

2

The Significance of the Matthean Temple Incident

THE PURPOSE OF THIS chapter is to grasp the significance of the Matthean temple incident (21:12–13) through the use of a method that I have described in the introduction as compositional analysis. Three steps will be taken in order to accomplish this. First, we will attempt to grasp the big picture of Matthew's Gospel by identifying its themes, emphases, and overall message. We will try to identify its author, date of writing, recipients, and occasion for writing, and approximate on the life setting of the intended readers. Second, we will discuss the immediate contexts of the temple incident, namely Jesus' entry into Jerusalem (21:1–11) and the healing, acclamation, and controversy in the temple (21:14–17). We will then analyze Matthew's account of the temple incident and identify its central message and key themes. Third, we will inquire how the temple incident fits into the overall narrative scheme of Matthew.

CONTEXTUAL CONSIDERATIONS[1]

Meaning is highly conditioned by context. Before we examine the temple incident itself, it is necessary to first determine its contexts, and this includes an inquiry into the overall message and emphasis of Matthew's

---

1. Refer to Appendix 1 for a summary of the contextual locations of the temple incident.

Gospel, as well as a study of the immediate contexts of the temple incident, such as what precedes and follows it.

Matthew's Overall Message and Emphasis

The Gospel of Matthew was written by a Jewish Christian for Jewish Christian readers with distinctively Jewish-Christian concerns. This chapter proceeds on the assumption of Matthean authorship.[2] The dual contexts of Judaism and the early church are most crucial for our understanding of Matthew's message. First, there is the background setting of the Jewish national and religious life and belief system. Matthew addresses a Jewish situation that has gone terribly wrong. The Jews continued to profess their identity as the chosen people of God, but this was almost an empty profession because it did not match reality. They were under the rule of pagan Rome. Jesus fundamentally differed from the Jews in interpreting this Roman subjugation. Whereas the Jews viewed it as the root problem, fueling revolutionary movements across Palestine,[3] Jesus viewed it as a result of the Jews' deeper problem of rebellion against God. This is the background why the Jews expected a political Messiah, and when Jesus did not turn out to be the one that they were hoping for, they rejected him and demanded his crucifixion.

Another aspect where the Jewish profession did not match reality is the degree of the failure of the Jews to live out the implications of their being the chosen people of God. As Nolland comments:

> Neither in terms of situation nor of behavior does the life experience of the Jewish people match the grand vision of restoration to be found in the OT prophets. Those who ought to have been providing spiritual leadership for the people are compromised in various ways and failing to provide the proper lead. A whole demonic empire is also active in the midst of the people: Satan has sown his *zizania* in the world; and individuals are in the grip of evil spirits."[4]

---

2. For perhaps the best defense of Matthean authorship, see Gundry, *Matthew*, 609–22.

3. See, e.g., Horsley, *Bandits*.

4. Nolland, *Gospel*, 39.

In view of these realities, Matthew presents Jesus as the Messiah, the Savior of his people from their sins.[5]

Second, there is the more specific, narrower setting of Jews converted to Jesus and now facing antagonism from former peers in Judaism. On the assumption that the Gospel author was Matthew the apostle, he himself as a Jewish Christian had presumably experienced the social, emotional, and intellectual struggles involved in his conversion from Judaism to Christianity. He could therefore write an account of Jesus' life and work that was specifically relevant to the needs of the Christian community that was undergoing the same tensions and struggles.[6]

What was the probable life setting of the Matthean community? Scholars have busied themselves with this question, and several reconstructions have been proposed.

First, some scholars[7] have suggested that the Matthean community consisted of Jewish Christians who were kicked out of the Jewish synagogues after the Council of Jamnia's issuance of *Birkath ha-Minim* sometime around 85 CE. *Birkath ha-Minim* was a phrase added into the Jewish synagogue benediction and believed to have been recited daily by the Jews. Its text was basically a curse, calling destruction on Christians and heretics alike.[8] Some scholars have taken this to be the pinnacle of Jewish antagonism towards Christianity, and they mark 85 CE to be the year when Christianity and Judaism parted ways.

Second, another group of scholars[9] have argued that, yes, the Matthean community consisted chiefly of Jewish Christians. But this reconstruction differs from the previous one in that it locates this community prior to 85 CE, when these Jewish Christians were supposedly still freely mingling with their Jewish counterparts in synagogues and other Jewish settings.

---

5. Consider, for instance, Matt 1:21.

6. As regards Gospel audiences, I remain of the view that the Gospels were written for specific, localized communities. I am not entirely convinced of Richard Bauckham's (*Gospels*) thesis that, in the first instance, the Gospels were written for *all Christians*. But an important contribution of Bauckham's proposal is the showing that the early Christian movement was not a scattering of isolated, somewhat hermetically sealed-off congregations.

7. Such as Stendahl, *School*; Strecker, "Concept"; Meier, *Vision*.

8. In the version found in Cairo Geniza, it reads, "Let Nazarenes [= Christians] and *minim* [= heretics] perish in a moment; let them be blotted out of the book of the living, and let them not be written with the righteous" (Carson and Moo, *Introduction*, 154).

9. Such as Hummel, *Auseinandersetzung*; Davies, *Setting*; Goulder, *Midrash*; Brown, "Community"; Barth, "Understanding."

The main weakness of these two reconstructions is that they are heavily indebted to the idea of a sharp rupture of Christian-Jewish relations in 85 CE. For one thing, we know very little about what really took place in the Council of Jamnia, and even the little that we know is debatable.[10] Second, the split that supposedly occurred in 85 CE does not mean that prior to this time Christians did not experience sharp opposition or being expelled from synagogues, nor does it imply that after 85 CE Christians, in response to their exclusion, totally stopped their outreach to the Judaist Jews.[11]

A third reconstruction is offered by still another group of scholars[12] who argue that the Matthean community was not only comfortably and happily located *inside* the Jewish synagogue but also that this community regarded the mission to the Gentiles as a peripheral option. However, no matter how these scholars try to base their position in the Matthean text, it is quite apparent that theirs is a one-sided reading of the evidence[13] and fails to explain the diverse material in the Gospel.[14]

In the midst of all these debates, what can we really know about the Matthean community? We have sufficient textual evidence[15] indicating that the Matthean community consisted chiefly of Jewish Christians. Other circumstantial details of our reconstruction will be based on that, and will also be affected by the date we assign to this Gospel. Whether this community were still active in the local Jewish synagogues or already kicked out, we cannot know with certainty. Certainly Matthew was concerned about them; he wrote this Gospel apparently to help them to know more about Jesus and strengthen their spiritual footing. It is likely that many if not most of these believers faced some kind of persecution, and such persecution might have emanated not from Roman authorities but from local synagogues and Jewish neighbors. Some of them might have been disowned by their families on account of their new faith which, during that time, was not only new but also heretical according to Jewish orthodoxy. The Jewish leadership had already rejected Jesus and had him crucified; how would any Jew who still

---

10. Hagner hypothesizes: "It may well be that [Jamnia] had no significance for the relationship between Jews and Christians" (*Matthew*, lxviii).

11. France, *Matthew*, 85–86, 98–102; France, *Gospel*, 14–19; Hagner, *Matthew*, lxv–lxxi.

12. Such as Overman, *Gospel*; Saldarini, *Community*; Sim, *Gospel*.

13. France, *Gospel*, 17.

14. Hagner, *Matthew*, lxv.

15. See Hagner, *Matthew*, lxiv–lxxi.

chose to convert to *this* Jesus be perceived by their fellow Jews? It would now be the burden of any Jesus-convert (who defected from Judaism) to make sense of their choice amidst the possible rejection, opposition, mockery, and shaming emanating from the left-behind Jewish family, friends, and synagogue. Maintaining contact with Jewish family and friends, not least evangelizing them, would have been extremely difficult. The Gospel of Matthew would have brought not only encouragement but also timely and much-needed theological education to these Jewish Christians. Craig Evans writes, "The evangelist was concerned to demonstrate that Jesus and his movement fulfill Jewish expectations and hopes and do not undermine the authoritative place of Torah."[16] Thus the Gospel of Matthew confirms "Jewish believers in the truth of Christianity as the fulfillment of the promises to Israel, which entails the argument that Jesus is the Messiah, that he was loyal to the law, and that he came to the Jews."[17]

The one word that best encapsulates the message of Matthew's Gospel is "fulfillment." First, this is directly stated in 5:17: "Do not think that I have come to abolish the law or the prophets; I have come not to abolish but to *fulfill*." Second, Matthew has as copious as 54 direct quotations from the OT and 262 allusions and verbal parallels.[18] Many of these "are explicitly concerned with the theme of fulfillment. . . . It is thus for Matthew not only the explicitly predictive portions of the OT that can be seen to be 'fulfilled' in Jesus, but also its historical characters, its narratives, and its cultic patterns, even the law itself (5:17; 11:13)."[19] Matthew's characteristic preface to many of these OT quotations is: "All this happened to fulfill what had been declared by the Lord through the prophet, who said . . ."[20]

---

16. Evans, "Book," 61.
17. Hagner, *Matthew*, lxx.
18. Based on the UBS *Greek New Testament*.
19. France, *Gospel*, 11.
20. Such as in 1:22 and repeated in 2:15, 17, 23; 4:14; 8:17; 12:17; 13:35; 21:4; 27:9—for a total of ten times. France indicates that most commentators agree to include 2:5 in the list, making it 11 in sum (*Gospel of Matthew*, 11). If we focus on the verb πληρόω, which all of the above ten passages share, then Matt 13:14–15 should also belong to the list. If we foreground the idea of fulfillment without using the word "fulfill," then Matt 3:3 should also be included. Hagner (*Matthew*, lv) notes that quotations employing the word γέγραπται can also stress fulfillment, as in 2:5, 11:10, and 26:31. Though without actual quotation, Matt 26:56 can also be stressing the fulfillment theme, as it says πληρωθῶσιν αἱ γραφαὶ τῶν προφητῶν ("in order that the writings of the prophets might be fulfilled").

The Significance of the Temple Incident in the Narratives of the Four Gospels

There has been much debate on the meaning of "fulfillment" (πληρῶσαι in 5:17).[21] But the fundamental meaning is straightforward: as the law and the prophets pointed to the coming of the Messiah, so in his coming (incarnation) Jesus the Messiah fulfilled them. Matthew sets forth Jesus as "Israel's royal Messiah (1:1; 19:28) in whom God's culminates and by whose words and life his followers—the true Israel (25:34)—may gain divine forgiveness and fellowship."[22] That this was Matthew's view is consistent with the repetitious occurrences of the fulfillment-of-prophecy formula. This central meaning does allow for corollary interpretations, such as that proposed by Hagner: Jesus fulfilled the law by bringing it to its intended meaning, by presenting a definitive interpretation of it, he being the Messiah and the ultimate interpreter of it.[23]

The Gospel of Matthew does not have markers that will allow for a comprehensive outline of the book. Some writers, for instance J. D. Kingsbury, have used the formula "From that time Jesus began to . . ." (4:17; 16:21) to mark out the main divisions, coming up with three main sections of the book: Jesus' person (1:1—4:16), Jesus' proclamation (4:17—16:20), and Jesus' passion (16:21—28:20).[24] Others, like D. R. Bauer, used the formula "And then, when Jesus had come to the end of these sayings . . ." (7:28; 11:1; 13:53; 19:1; 26:1), coming up with five divisions of the book.[25] France uses a geographical framework to divide Matthew into four parts including

---

21. Davies and Allison (*Matthew*, 3:485–88) list nine proposed interpretations: (1) as a translation of ōsîp, "to add to"; (2) as the equivalent of the Aramaic qûm, "to establish," "to make valid," "to bring into effect"; (3) as in Rom 8:4, "to obey"; (4) "Jesus fulfills the law by observing it perfectly and completely in his own person and ministry"; (5) "Jesus fulfills or completes the law by bringing a new law which transcends the old"; (6) "The Torah is fulfilled when Jesus, explaining God's original intention, brings out its perfect or inner meaning and expands and extends its demands"; (7) "Jesus fulfills the law because, through his coming, he enables others to meet the Torah's demands"; (8) "When Jesus fulfills the law or the prophets, he does it by bringing the new righteousness, which is the new spirit of love: love is the fulfilling of the law"; and (9) "The fulfillment is eschatological: the *telos* which the Torah anticipated, namely, the Messiah, has come and revealed the law's definitive meaning. Prophecy has been realized." Not all of these proposed interpretations are correct; in my view 3, 4, 8, and 9 are acceptable interpretations (though not of equal importance) and should be combined to provide a rich view of the Matthean meaning of Jesus' fulfilling the law.

22. Metzger, in *NOAB*, 1.

23. Hagner, *Matthew*, 104–6.

24. Kingsbury, *Matthew*.

25. Bauer, *Structure*.

the prologue: prologue (1:1—4:11), in Galilee (4:12—16:20), from Galilee to Jerusalem (16:21—20:34), and in Jerusalem (21:1—28:15).[26]

The difficulty that attends the structuring of Matthew does not pose difficulty to this research. In the three outlines cited above, scholars are unanimous in putting the temple incident in the final division; that is, toward Jesus' passion week, happening in Jerusalem.

What Goes Before

It is helpful to describe briefly here the chronology of Jesus' life from the time that he began his public ministry up to the time when he entered Jerusalem for his passion week. Two questions need to be answered. First, how many years was Jesus' public ministry? Second, how many journeys did he embark on during his public ministry? To answer the first question, the obvious starting point is his baptism and the end point is his final week in Jerusalem. Based on the accounts of the four Gospels, between these two points are at least three Passovers. The first is mentioned in John 2:13, happening shortly after Jesus' baptism. The second Passover is mentioned in John 4:45, paralleled in Mark 1:14 and Luke 4:14. The third Passover is mentioned in John 11:55, and this is the Passover coinciding with Jesus' passion week. From this we can conclude that Jesus' public ministry lasted for about three years.

The answer to the second question can be reckoned geographically, with a total of nine journeys. The first six journeys were concentrated in Galilee with Capernaum as the home base, and the last three bring Jesus to Judea without any pronounced central point.[27]

The Message of Matthew 21

In Matthew's narrative, the temple incident happens right after Jesus' entrance to Jerusalem ("then," v. 12) and right before his acts of healing in the temple (v. 14).[28] Why does Matthew arrange his materials in this particular

---

26. France, *Gospel*.

27. Maas, "Chronology," online.

28. Luke also places the temple incident (19:45–46) right after Jesus' triumphal entry into Jerusalem (19:28–44), though unlike Matthew, who refers to Jesus' acts of healing in the temple following the temple incident, Luke only refers to Jesus' teaching in the temple (19:47–48). Mark and John significantly differ from Matthew's account. Mark

way? What did he wish to convey by this? Let us examine his presentation of Jesus' entry into Jerusalem (21:1–11) and acts of healing in the temple (vv. 14–17).

Jesus' Entry into Jerusalem (21:1–11)

The Scripture Is Fulfilled

What stands out in Matthew's account of Jesus' entry into Jerusalem is his comment in verse 4: "This took place to fulfill what had been spoken through the prophet." This fulfillment-of-the-Scriptures motif is widely emphasized in Matthew and is crucial to identifying his authorial purposes for reporting Jesus' entry to Jerusalem and his meaning for the temple incident. What does Matthew say was a fulfillment of the Scriptures? Is it Jesus' sending his two disciples to fetch the donkey,[29] or is it the entry itself? Gundry thinks that it is not the triumphal entry because at this point in the narrative Jesus has not yet entered Jerusalem. Instead, Gundry argues, Matthew refers to Jesus' sending his two disciples to fetch the donkey as fulfilling the scriptures.[30] If we limit our consideration to the chronology of events, specifically the progression of verses 1–4, then Gundry's proposal would be correct and it would then be incorrect to say that Jesus' triumphal entry fulfills the scriptures. But then we also need to ask which scriptures Matthew thinks are being fulfilled.

In verse 4, Matthew mentions "the prophet," then in verse 5 he quotes from that prophet: "Tell the daughter of Zion, 'Look, your king is coming to you, humble, and mounted on a donkey, and on a colt, the foal of a donkey.'" It is clear that Matthew is here quoting Zech 9:9, where it is written: "Rejoice greatly, O daughter of Zion! Shout aloud, O daughter of Jerusalem! Lo, your king comes to you; triumphant and victorious is he, humble and

---

sandwiches the temple incident (11:15–19) between the cursing (11:12–14) and withering (11:20–25) of the fig tree. John markedly differs from the Synoptic evangelists, for he presents the temple incident (2:13–22) as Jesus' first act in Jerusalem after the first public miracle of turning water into wine in Cana (2:1–11).

29. Matt 21:7 says that Jesus sends his two disciples to fetch two animals—a donkey and her colt. Matthew is unique in this for Mark, Luke, and John all referred to only one animal. According to *NOAB* the Hebrew word used in Zech 9:9 meant one animal, not two (p. 1227, OT), and that Matthew's reference to two animals "may have arisen through misunderstanding the form of Hebrew poetic expression in Zech. 9:9" (p. 31, NT).

30. Gundry, *Matthew*, 410.

riding on a donkey, on a colt, the foal of a donkey." We must note that Matthew replaces "Rejoice greatly, O daughter of Zion" of Zech 9:9 with "Tell the daughter of Zion," which is from Isa 62:11. Both of these OT texts do not simply refer to the fetching of the animal but also, and primarily, to the Messiah's entry into Jerusalem. In light of this, the Matthean fulfillment motif in 21:4 is perhaps better understood as applying to the whole triumphal entry, including the fetching of the animal.

Jesus the Messiah-King Enters Jerusalem

Besides presenting Jesus' entry into Jerusalem as a fulfillment of the Scriptures, Matthew shows that Jesus enters Jerusalem as the Messiah-King, and this is supported by the following considerations. Firstly, there is messianic import to Matthew's mention of the Mount of Olives in 21:1.[31] France thinks that this is not only for the sake of geographical clarity that Matthew mentions the Mouth of Olives in addition to Bethphage.[32] Zechariah 14:4 (see also Ezek 11:23; 43:2) declares that the LORD ("Yahweh") will stand on the Mount of Olives, which is "east of Jerusalem." Hagner says that it is perhaps for these messianic associations of the Mouth of Olives that Jesus chose this place for his ascension and his return "when the eschaton is fully and finally to dawn."[33]

Secondly, for Matthew, in 21:5 Jesus' riding on a donkey was a fulfillment of Zech 9:9. This OT text, including verse 10, is a messianic prophecy predicting the coming of a gentle and meek king who comes to Jerusalem and establishes universal peace and worldwide dominion. Jesus is the Messiah-King and he fulfills the prophecy. But he is not the sort of a militaristic Messiah that patriotic Jews have anticipated and hoped for. Furthermore, the messianic prophecy of Zech 9:9 has an underlying royal ideology. The historical basis of this prophecy was the "story of David's return to the city after the defeat of Absalom's rebellion, when [David] came in triumph as king, and yet humbly and in peace (2 Sam 19–20). When the Son of David chose to ride down to the city from the Mount of Olives on a donkey, the acted allusion was unmistakable."[34]

---

31. The mention of the Mount of Olives is not unique to Matthew but is shared with Mark and Luke.
32. France, *Gospel*, 775.
33. Hagner, *Matthew*, 593.
34. France, *Gospel*, 773–74.

Thirdly, the title "the Son of David" is ascribed to Jesus by the crowds: "Hosanna to the Son of David!" (21:9). This ascription is uniquely Matthean. Mark has the word "kingdom" in the crowd's acclamation of Jesus: "Blessed is the coming kingdom of our ancestor David!" (11:10a). Luke and John have the word "king": "Blessed is the king who comes in the name of the Lord!" (Luke 19:38a). "Blessed is the one who comes in the name of the Lord—the King of Israel!" (John 12:13b). The title "Son of David" is a favorite of Matthew's, which occurs ten times in this Gospel, compared to four times each in Mark and Luke. This title has reference to the royal figure, the Messiah, of 2 Sam 7:12–16, "who would assume the throne of David . . . thereby inaugurating a kingdom of perfection and righteousness that would last forever."[35] For Matthew and the accompanying crowds, Jesus is the Messiah-King that the prophets had prophesied, and now he comes to Jerusalem, the city of David, and so they are jubilant.

Besides the many important details we find in 21:1–11,[36] there are two firsts that Matthew's account of Jesus' entry into Jerusalem foregrounds.[37] Firstly, for the first time through his actions (not words) Jesus publicly claims to be the Messiah and in fact presents himself as such to the people of Jerusalem. He breaks the messianic secrecy that he had observed prior to this time. Even when he was in Jericho, he did not quiet the two blind men who were shouting, calling him the Son of David. This time, when the huge crowds shouted "Hosanna to the Son of David," he did not rebuke them but rather deliberately provoked them. What is more, his decision to enter Jerusalem riding on a donkey could not have been because of physical necessity. He had already walked hundreds of miles from the northern Galilee and having arrived at Bethphage he was already in the vicinity of the holy city. But Jesus did not come "to slip quietly into Jerusalem";[38] he did not come simply as any ordinary Galilean pilgrim. He came as the Messiah, the King of the Jews.

Second, for the first time we have a record of crowds acclaiming Jesus as the Son of David, acknowledging his kingship. We read in 20:29 that

---

35. Hagner, *Matthew*, 9.

36. Davies and Allison (*Matthew*, 3:112): the theme of prophetic fulfillment (vv. 4–5; see also 1:22–23; etc), Jesus' trek to Jerusalem (vv. 1, 10; see also 16:21; 20:17), his "meekness" (v. 4; see also 11:29), and his status as "king" (v. 5; see also 2:1–12), "Son of David" (v. 9; see also 1:1–18), "the coming one" (v. 9; see also 3:11; 11:3), and "prophet" (v. 11; see also 13:57).

37. Davies and Allison, *Matthew*.

38. France, *Gospel*, 774.

there was a large crowd accompanying Jesus to Jerusalem. Presumably they were pilgrims en route to Jerusalem for the Passover feast, not necessarily disciples of Jesus.[39] "Their proud identification of him as 'the prophet from Galilee' (21:11) indicates that the majority of this crowd, like Jesus and his immediate followers, were Galileans making their regular pilgrimage to Jerusalem."[40] This crowd becomes a "huge crowd" in 21:8. It is now this huge crowd that, in Bethphage, while Jesus was riding on a donkey, "spread their cloaks on the road, while others cut branches from the trees and spread them on the road. The crowds that went ahead of him and those that followed him shouted, 'Hosanna to the Son of David! Blessed is he who comes in the name of the Lord! Hosanna in the highest!'" (21:8-9).[41]

Jesus came to Jerusalem as the Messiah, the Son of David, the King of the Jews, and the pilgrim crowds hailed him as such. His unmistakably messianic gestures and postures and the jubilant acclamations of the huge crowds clearly laid down the challenge in front of the Jews of the holy city. Matthew records in 21:10 that the whole city was stirred (lit. "shaken") and asked, "Who is this?"[42]—not a curious but an antagonistic question, anticipating the decisive confrontation that would ensue, which as we know would culminate in Jesus' death on the cross.

Healing, Acclamation, and Controversy (21:14-17)

In Matthew's account, Jesus' protest in the temple is immediately followed by the accounts of a healing activity,[43] children praising him, and an exchange between him and the chief priests and the teachers of the law, which is not shared by the other Gospels.

39. Matthew many times speaks of crowds following Jesus, but not necessarily believing in him (4:23; 8:1; 12:15; 14:13; 19:2).

40. France, *Gospel*, 765.

41. France has called attention to the mistake that many Bible interpreters commit: equating the crowds that acclaimed Jesus as the Son of David and the crowds that demanded his crucifixion. They are different crowds—the crowds demanding Jesus' crucifixion being primarily Judeans particularly Jerusalemites (*Gospel*, 773).

42. Davies and Allison note the irony here: "The daughter of Zion, for whose sake Jesus comes, does not comprehend the tumult before her gates or understand that her king has come and that prophecy has been fulfilled . . . As Jesus leaves the sympathetic pilgrims to encounter the hostility of the holy city he is exchanging his royal mount for a criminal's cross. His exit will not be as his entrance" (*Matthew*, 3:128-29).

43. This is Jesus' last healing in Jerusalem as recorded by Matthew, whereas Mark does not record any miracle of Jesus in Jerusalem.

What Matthew is doing here is similar to what he does in 21:10–11, where he documents the reaction of the Jerusalem residents to Jesus' arrival. Without putting a break to the narrative of the temple incident, Matthew reports in verse 14: "The blind and the lame came to him at the temple, and he healed them." The brevity of this report is noteworthy and quite specific ("the blind and the lame") compared to the more general reports of healing (e.g., "all who were ill," "the sick") recorded in 4:23–24; 8:16; 9:35; 12:15; 14:14; 15:30–31; and 19:2.[44]

Matthew does not say how and why the blind and the blame were allowed into the temple. It should be noted that the Jewish custom of the time restricted their access to the temple significantly.[45] Second Samuel 5:8 says that "the blind and lame shall not come into the house."[46] In Lev 21:16–20, the blind and lame are mentioned in the list of those prohibited from entering God's sanctuary. As Repschinski points out, contemporary sources from the Qumran community are even more restrictive: they do not allow the maimed any participation in the community of the saved.[47] For instance, 1 QS 2:5–22 says:

> And no man smitten with any human uncleanness shall enter the assembly of God; no man smitten with any of them shall be confirmed in his office in his congregation. No man smitten in his flesh, or paralyzed in his feet or hands, or lame, or blind, or deaf, or dumb, or smitten in his flesh with a visible blemish; no old and tottery man unable to stay still in the midst of the congregation; none of these shall come to hold office among the congregation of the men of renown, for the Angels of Holiness are with their congregation.[48]

By healing the blind and the lame who came to him in the temple, Jesus the Son of David is unlike King David of old. If the Jewish customs would not allow the blind and the lame in the temple, not only did Jesus welcome

---

44. France, *Gospel*, 788.

45. Repschinski, *Stories*, 188.

46. Apparently this saying was born out of David's order to his troops stated in 2 Sam 5:8a: "Whoever would strike down the Jebusites, let him get up the water shaft to attack the lame and the blind, those who David hates." These are not the lame and blind among the Jewish people but among the Jebusites. David came to hate them because when he was attacking the Jebusites to conquer them, they said to him: "You will not get in here; even the blind and the lame can ward you off" (2 Sam 6:6b).

47. Repschinski, *Stories*, 188 n. 9.

48. See also 1QM 7.5–6; CD 15.15–17.

them there, he healed them there! The therapeutic Son of David[49] turned the temple into a house of healing, restoring it to its rightful purpose.

Besides the healing, Matthew also records the reaction of the chief priests and the scribes (first mentioned in 2:4) to the wonders (τὰ θαυμάσια[50]) that Jesus performed and to the children's acclamation of Jesus: they were indignant (ἠγανάκτησαν). θαυμάσια is an NT *hapax legomenon* and Matthew's use of it to refer to the healing is rather unprecedented, for normally as in the rest of his Gospel he uses δυνάμεις to refer to miracles. This observation led Repschinski to surmise that θαυμάσια does not only refer to Jesus' healing of the blind and the lame but also to his protest in the temple.[51]

Most commentators, however, limit the reference to the healing.[52] What incensed the chief priests and the scribes, however, was not the healings but primarily the children's acclamation of Jesus. The children were shouting "Hosanna to the Son of David." These children might be part of the pilgrim crowds who earlier shouted the same acclaim to Jesus outside the city gates. The Jewish leaders had heard enough of their shouts and instead of directly rebuking them, which they could have done, they went to tell Jesus to rebuke the children. They complained to him: "Do you hear *what* these children are saying?" They were incensed by the children's calling Jesus the Son of David, for it sounded so blasphemous to their ears. "Son of David" refers only to the prophesied Messiah-King who would come, and to ascribe it to Jesus was not only inappropriate but also blasphemous, the Jewish leaders would have thought. Jesus' reply is yes, and in so doing he defends the children and by implication he accepts their acclamation—that he is the Son of David—and offers a scriptural basis for it by quoting Psalm 8:3 (LXX), a psalm written by David: "From the mouth of babes and those who suckle I will bring forth praise." France explains:

> The psalm speaks of how God the creator silences his enemies by means of "strength" (so the Hebrew) which comes from the mouths of children. "Strength" is often ascribed to God in a formula of praise . . . and when that "strength" issues from mouths it is not hard to see why LXX translated it as "praise." The most

---

49. On this see Duling, "Son of David"; Loader, "Son of David."

50. This is the only occurrence of this word in the NT.

51. Repschinski, *Stories*, 189–90.

52. E.g., Davies and Allison, *Matthew*, 3:141; France, *Gospel*, 788; Hagner, *Matthew*, 599; Gundry, *Matthew*, 413.

striking feature of this quotation is . . . the bold assumption by Jesus that what the psalm says about the praise of *God* (in distinction from mere human beings, Ps 8:4) is applicable to the children's praise of *him*.[53]

ANALYSIS OF THE TEMPLE INCIDENT PERICOPE (21:12-13)[54]

Greek text:

> 12 Καὶ εἰσῆλθεν Ἰησοῦς εἰς τὸ ἱερόν τοῦ θεοῦ, καὶ ἐξέβαλεν πάντας τοὺς πωλοῦντας καὶ ἀγοράζοντας ἐν τῷ ἱερῷ, καὶ τὰς τραπέζας τῶν κολλυβιστῶν κατέστρεψεν καὶ τὰς καθέδρας τῶν πωλούντων τὰς περιστεράς, 13 καὶ λέγει αὐτοῖς, Γέγραπται, Ὁ οἶκός μου οἶκος προσευχῆς κληθήσεται, ὑμεῖς δὲ αὐτὸν ποιεῖτε σπήλαιον λῃστῶν.

Translation:

> 12 Then Jesus entered the temple and drove out all who were selling and buying in the temple, and he overturned the tables of the money-changers and the seats of those who sold doves. 13 He said to them: "It is written: 'My house shall be called a house of prayer'; but you are making it a den of robbers."

Jesus' action can be divided into three parts:

1. He enters the temple area (v. 12a).
2. He drives out all who are buying and selling there (v. 12b). He overturns the tables of the money-changers and the benches of those selling doves (v. 12c).
3. He appeals to Scriptures (v. 13).

It is helpful to note once again that in Matthew's chronology, Jesus' entry into Jerusalem and his protest in the temple courts are recounted as happening on the same day (in contrast to Mark's where there is a day's interval). The first thing that Jesus does in Jerusalem is enter the temple and perform his dramatic act there. Things happen very fast, adding to their urgent and dramatic nature. Matthew's uninterrupted reporting of these two

---

53. France, *Gospel*, 789.

54. Refer to Appendix 2 for a comparison of the Synoptic Gospels' accounts of the temple incident.

events "has the effect of emphasizing the identity of the one who now enters the temple: it is the messianic king,[55] the Son of David."[56] It also means that Matthew intended for us to view Jesus' entry into Jerusalem in light of the temple incident and vice versa.

Jesus Enters the Temple

Matthew names Jesus in verse 12a, καὶ εἰσῆλθεν Ἰησοῦς εἰς τὸ ἱερόν ("and when Jesus came into the temple"). This is of course necessitated by verses 10–11. Mark and Luke do not name Jesus because it seems unnecessary as they do not have the equivalent of Matt 21:10–11. Τὸ ἱερόν literally refers to the whole temple complex,[57] but the context here limits its meaning to the Court of the Gentiles (or "the temple courtyard") into which Gentile converts to Judaism were allowed. Davies and Allison describe this place as "the large enclosure which surrounded the court of women and the court of priests."[58] According to France,

> The majority of the huge temple complex (about 13.5 hectares, thirty-acres, roughly six times the size of Trafalgar Square) consisted of this open space, nearly a mile in circumference, surrounding the temple building and its inner courtyards and itself surrounded by porticoes, into which anyone could go so long as they did not pass the barriers which restricted the central area to Jews. It formed the natural meeting place for visitors and locals alike, especially at festival seasons, and the porticoes provided shaded areas for groups to gather and for teachers to collect a crowd, and in the days before the Passover also for the flourishing market in sacrificial animals and sacred money. When Jesus "taught in the temple," he may well have been one of several such teachers, but he was in the place where people in general could best be reached.[59]

55. Kinman's ("Entry") conclusion that Jesus' entry was a royal but not a messianic event should be read in light of his specific definition of messianism, which he views as an armed struggle against Israel's oppressors, the Romans. Yes, Jesus did not enter Jerusalem to lead an armed rebellion against Rome. But Kinman is wrong, for Jesus did enter Jerusalem as the Messiah-King to liberate his people from their sins (see, e.g., Matt 1:21).

56. Hagner, *Matthew*, 600.

57. Ναός is the other term that is used of the temple with a specific reference to the sanctuary.

58. Davies and Allison, *Matthew*, 3:137.

59. France, *Gospel*, 770–71.

So it is important to keep in mind where Jesus' dramatic act took place: not in the sanctuary but in the temple complex, a very huge area, which transforms into a marketplace during festival seasons. Majority of scholars reckon the timing of Jesus' entry to Jerusalem and the temple act as during the Passover season, at the outset of the passion week.[60]

Jesus Drives Out the Sellers and Buyers

The first thing that Jesus does upon arriving in Jerusalem is to enter the temple[61]—that is, the Court of the Gentiles. And look what he finds: a marketplace! Right away the evangelist tells us: Ἰησοῦς . . . ἐξέβαλεν πάντας τοὺς πωλοῦντας καὶ ἀγοράζοντας ἐν τῷ ἱερῷ ("Jesus . . . drove out all who were buying and selling there") (v. 12a). What is remarkable here is Jesus' sense of freedom, responsibility, and urgency to act in response to what he perceived as a misuse (and/or abuse) of the temple. He did not inquire with the temple authorities about the problem, nor did he ask their permission for his public protest. He was bold, authoritative, and passionate.

Matthew says that Jesus ἐξέβαλεν (lit. "threw out" or "cast out") all who were selling and buying in the temple. The word ἐξέβαλεν is common to all the four Gospels. The translation "threw out" is a rather strong language, suggestive of violence.[62] The idea of "drove out" borne out by newer translations such as the NIV seems more preferable. Jesus drove out of the temple τοὺς πωλοῦντας ("the sellers") and ἀγοράζοντας ("buyers"). The sellers sold provisions for sacrificial worship like animals and birds intended especially for pilgrim worshipers to buy. Money-exchange services were also offered for customers who needed to exchange their Greco-Roman monies for Tyrian coins, which alone could be used in making offerings or paying the temple tax.[63] The phrase πάντας τοὺς πωλοῦντας καὶ ἀγοράζοντας may

---

60. A few other scholars argue in favor of the feast of Tabernacles: Manson, "Cleansing"; Smith, "Time"; Smith, "Tabernacles."

61. The temple was of course central to Jewish ideology. "It was not only the focus of the nation's religious life, but also a symbol of national identity and pride" (France, *Gospel*, 782). For a detailed description of the temple and its significance, see Wright, *New Testament*, 224–26; Wright, *Jesus*, 406–12.

62. Davies and Allison, *Matthew*, 3:137.

63. Hagner, *Matthew*, 600.

refer to all kinds of commercial activities happening in the temple where the temple treasurers and their staff were involved.[64]

He Overturns the Tables of the Moneychangers and the Benches of Those Selling Doves

As has been noted above, the temple courtyard (the "Court of the Gentiles") became a marketplace especially during seasons of Jewish national feasts, like the Passover. Animals and doves were sold and money-exchange services were provided in the temple precincts especially for pilgrim worshipers who came from the provinces and needed to buy animal offerings and the acceptable form of currency to pay for the temple tax. For us to further grasp what was really going on, the following points are crucial.

First, the system of buying and selling and money exchange in the temple courtyard was not a private enterprise of certain businessmen but a facility organized by the temple treasury.[65] It was designed and operated not only to provide services to worshipers but also to generate income for the temple.[66] Second, there are indications in early documents to the abusive and exploitative nature of this system. One clue may be found in Matthew's mention of the sellers of doves, whose seats Jesus overturned. Some scholars are of the view that the temple treasurers monopolized the sale of doves (which was not the case with cattle, sheep, and goats). Doves were the sacrificial offerings of the poor (see, for example, *m. Ker.* 6:8; Josephus, *A.J.* 3:230). Consider one evidence from the Mishnah as to the exorbitant price the doves were sold at one point:

> It happened that the price of pigeons in Jerusalem reached the value of golden dinars and Rabbi Simeon ben Gamaliel exclaimed—"I swear by this Temple that I shall not sleep the night until the price comes down to silver dinars." He went into the [temple] court

---

64. Bauckham further argues that the buyers did not include worshipers, for why would Jesus drive out worshipers? Rather, "they could include temple staff buying in supplies for the temple and merchants purchasing valuable items which people had donated to the temple" ("Demonstration," 78). This suggestion seems plausible, though its problem is that it gives no room for those pilgrim-worshipers who needed to buy sacrificial animals or exchange their Roman monies for the accepted Tyrian ones.

65. Bauckham, "Demonstration," 75.

66. Bauckham ("Demonstration," 78). Borg writes, "Both the moneychangers and sellers of birds were part of the temple system that stood at the center of the tributary mode of production, drawing money to the Jerusalem elites" (*Jesus*, 114).

> and proclaimed: "A woman who owes five certain birth sacrifices or five certain sightings of menstrual blood need bring only one sacrifice. She will then be pure enough to eat of all sacrifices ..." Immediately the price fell to one fourth of a silver dinar.[67]

The rabbi referenced in this story was Simeon son of Gamaliel I, a Pharisee whom Josephus credited with being an influential member of the Sanhedrin prior to the fall of Jerusalem (*Vita* 189–96). He thought that the price of doves was too high and he sought to reduce it. Considering that doves were the sacrificial offerings of the poor, we have here an indication of a system that was unfavorable to and exploitative of the poor.

Let us combine the two together—the money-changers and dove-sellers—and inquire about the conduct of the temple leadership. There is a piece of evidence, a lament, found in *b. Pesaḥ* 57a, whose text goes like this:

> Woe unto me because of the house of Baithos [Boethus]; Woe unto me for their lances [or 'evil-speaking']!
>
> Woe unto me because of the house of Hanin [=Annas (NT) and Ananus (Josephus)],
>
> Woe unto me for their whisperings [or 'calumnies']!
> Woe unto me because of their reed pens!
>
> Woe unto me because of the house of Ishmael b. Phiabi, Woe unto me because of their fist!
>
> For they are high priests and their sons are treasurers and their sons-in-law are temple overseers,
>
> and their servants smite the people with sticks.

Bauckham affirms that this is an authentic lament dating to before the fall of Jerusalem. It mentions four families that "supplied most of the high priests from the reign of Herod the Great to the fall of Jerusalem, and the lament must intend to refer to the activities of these four families over a period from at least ca. 6 BCE to at least 60 CE."[68] It accuses the priestly aristocracy of intrigue, nepotism, and violence. The seventh chapter of the *T. Mos.* could also be cited, for it describes the priests as living like princes (7:8–10) and accuses them of luxurious and gluttonous living financed by ill-gotten wealth.[69]

---

67. See also *m. Ker.* 1:7.
68. Bauckham, "Demonstration," 79.
69. See further evidence in Bauckham, "Demonstration," 80–81. Evans ("Action," 263), after citing a large body of evidence, writes: "Various groups, such as some tannaitic

The Significance of the Matthean Temple Incident

It is in this context, plus taking into consideration his identity, that we must attempt to understand Jesus' overturning of the money-changers' tables and the dove-sellers' benches. The traditional proposal that Jesus' action was an act of cleansing is apparently not a viable option, for Jesus did not perform any temple cleansing, and if ever he did then he failed because the mercantile activities went on until the temple's destruction. The proposal advanced by Sanders, that Jesus' overturning tables signified the coming destruction of the temple and its replacement by another, also appears deficient, for it necessarily makes Jesus oblivious or ambivalent to the abuses we have just noted above.

At the very basic level, Jesus' action was clearly a protest, a demonstration. "It was an indictment of what the temple had become: the center of an economically exploitative system dominated by the ruling elites and legitimized by an ideology of purity grounded in an interpretation of Scripture."[70] Then, at the eschatological level, we can accept Sanders's interpretation—that Jesus' act was a portent of the temple's upcoming destruction. These two levels of interpretation are consistent with the portrait of Jesus that Matthew has been painting: he is the Messiah-King who by his words and deeds fulfills the Scriptures.

Jesus Appeals to Scriptures

Jesus justifies his actions by quoting and alluding to, respectively, two OT Scriptures. These serve as our compass in locating the reason why Jesus has done what he has done. He begins by saying Γέγραπται ("it is written"[71]), which is a common introductory formula. The first text is Isa 56:7, quoted almost verbatim from the LXX except that in Matthew's account Jesus leaves out the words πᾶσιν τοῖς ἔθνεσιν.[72] Then he alludes to Jer 7:11 with

---

and early amoraic rabbis, the zealots, Qumran sectarians, and Josephus viewed various priests, High Priests, or priestly families as wealthy, corrupt, often greedy, and sometimes violent."

70. Borg, *Jesus*, 114.

71. Or "it stands written" (Hagner, *Matthew*, 65).

72. M. Eugene Boring ("Gospel") finds Matthew's leaving this phrase to be "surprising, since Matthew advocates the post-Easter Gentile mission of his own church (28:18–20), but is understandable on closer reflection. Mathew has no interest in criticizing Judaism for its purported lack of openness to Gentiles; he is, in fact, sarcastic and critical of the Pharisees' Gentile mission (23:15)." Then Boring agrees with our analysis that Matthew's dropping the phrase was because he wanted to contrast "house of prayer"

the words "den of robbers." Combining these two, Matthew records: "It is written, 'My house shall be called a house of prayer; but you are making it a 'den of robbers.'"

The Matthean Jesus has purposefully, meaningfully, and creatively juxtaposed these two OT texts in order to not only explain and justify his actions but also to lay a charge against the temple leadership. By quoting Isa 56:7, Jesus tells his audience of God's intention for the temple: for it to be a house of prayer. By alluding to Jer 7:11, Jesus indicts the temple leadership of the crime of making the temple a den of robbers. In short, the temple leadership has failed in its calling. That is the judgment of Jesus, the Messiah-King.

Transparently, Matthew's central interest in Isa 56 is in the temple being an οἶκος προσευχῆς, not so much its being a house of prayer for all peoples (πᾶσιν τοῖς ἔθνεσιν).[73] That the temple is preeminently the place of prayer is not new or surprising.[74] King Solomon in his dedicatory prayer for the temple mentioned repeatedly something to this effect: "When your people turn to you, praying and making supplication to you in this temple, then hear from heaven . . ." (1 Kgs 33:53). Other texts tell us that the Jews went to the temple to pray: 3 Macc 2:10; 2 Macc 10:26; Sir 51:14; Luke 2:37; 18:10. Moreover, as Bauckham observes in connection with Isa 56:7:

> The sacrifices were regarded as expressions of prayer and were intended to be accompanied by prayer (1 Bar. 1:10–14; Josephus, *C. Ap.* 2:196; see also Neh 11:17) . . . In using the term "house of prayer," therefore, Jesus was not rejecting or downplaying the sacrificial cult. Rather he was insisting on its purpose: to be the expression of the prayer of those who came to the temple to worship. It was this real purpose of the sacrificial cult which was being frustrated by the temple authorities when they made it a means of financial exaction.[75]

---

and "den of thieves" more sharply (p. 406).

73. πᾶσιν τοῖς ἔθνεσιν is quite central to Isa 56. Twice in this chapter the word "foreigner" has been mentioned, both instances speaking of foreigners binding themselves to the LORD, and God gives them the promise in verse 7 saying: "These I will bring to my holy mountain and give them joy in my house of prayer . . ." And then πᾶσιν τοῖς ἔθνεσιν occurs again in the latter part of verse 7. That Matthew left this phrase out enhances his focus on the temple being a house of prayer.

74. Bauckham, "Demonstration," 83–84.

75. Bauckham, "Demonstration," 84.

The opposite of the temple's being an οἶκος προσευχῆς is its being an σπήλαιον λῃστῶν ("den of robbers"), an allusion to Jer 7:11. Following other scholars, N. T. Wright rules out the idea of "thief" or "robber" as the meaning the Greek λῃστής and its Hebrew equivalent *parisim*, and settles instead with the sense of bandits, guerillas, and revolutionaries against Rome.[76] For Wright, the temple had become a "den of robbers" by becoming "the focal point of the hope of national liberation . . . the talisman of nationalist violence."[77] For two reasons, Wright's conclusion is hard to accept. First, we are not sure how much the priestly aristocracy, who were enjoying the status quo, were involved in the nationalist struggle against Rome. Second, Wright's politicized conclusion fails to sufficiently account for the moral and spiritual dimensions of the problem that Jesus wanted to attack.

There is more than enough textual evidence that regard the temple priests and authorities as robbers and thieves. The Babylonian Talmud (see *b. Pesaḥ* 57a) tells about the servants of the chief priests who beat people with sticks, taking by force more than their fair share of the tithes and offerings. The Jeremiah targum in particular contains a number of relevant texts. For instance, *Tg. Jer.* 7:11 substitutes "synagogue of the wicked" for the Hebrew text's "den of robbers." *Tg. Jer.* 7:9 specifically calls the religious leaders "thieves." *Tg. Jer.* 8:10 describes the religious leaders as "robbers of money." *Tg. Jer.* 23:11 accuses the priests of having "stolen their ways," instead of being "godly."

In sum, in Jeremiah targum the priests "are accused of robbery, being overly concerned about money, failing to inquire of God or showing compassion for the sick, and of having lack of concern for the people."[78] The temple has become a den of robbers in the sense that the priests "treat the temple . . . as a base from which they go out on marauding raids and to which they return with the loot . . . The priestly aristocracy, by virtue of their control of the temple hierarchy occupy positions of privilege and unassailable authority, are abusing these positions as means of plundering the people."[79]

---

76. Wright, *Jesus*, 419.

77. Wright, *Jesus*, 419. One can readily see Wright's indebtedness to Marcus Borg's conclusions.

78. Evans, "Action," 269.

79. Bauckham, "Demonstration," 84.

SUMMARY AND CONCLUSION

We have noted above significant aspects of Matthew's account of the temple incident, aspects that have direct bearing on its interpretation. First, the uninterrupted flow of the report beginning with Jesus entry into Jerusalem (21:1–11) and the temple incident (21:12–13) indicates that one will shed light on the meaning of the other. For instance, Matthew takes pain to show that Jesus is the Messiah-King and it is as such that he enters Jerusalem. Matthew also shows that Jesus' entry into Jerusalem as the Messiah-King is the fulfillment of the Scriptures. Because of the noted continuity, it is highly likely that Matthew would like us to find these themes also in the temple incident account.

Second, we also noted Matthew's apparent emphasis on the temple as οἶκος προσευχῆς ("house of prayer"). This is clear not only from Matthew's leaving out the words πᾶσιν τοῖς ἔθνεσιν ("to the Gentiles") in quoting Isa 56:7, but also from his exclusive report of Jesus' healing the blind and lame in the temple (21:14–17). Jesus highlights the contrast between what God had originally intended for the temple—as οἶκος προσευχῆς—and what the ruling priests had made of the temple—σπήλαιον λῃστῶν ("den of robbers")—and his healing of the blind and lame who came to him in the temple is an immediate, albeit only momentary, fulfillment of God's intention for the temple. Jesus had made the temple indeed a house of prayer. Hence we are to view Jesus—in his entrance into Jerusalem, in his protest in the temple, and in his other actuations in Matthew's Gospel—as the royal Messiah who not only knows who he is but also, particularly in his twin acts of entering Jerusalem and the temple, anxious to present himself as such to the Jews. His protest in the temple is therefore as royal and messianic as his entry to Jerusalem. This picture militates against interpreting Jesus' temple act in a rather strait-jacketed fashion or in inflexible either/or way. The basic weakness of E. P. Sanders's proposal—that Jesus' temple act was a portent for the upcoming destruction of the temple—was not that it was wrong; it missed the other aspects of Jesus motivations. That the temple act was a token of the forthcoming destruction of the temple is consistent with Jesus' identity as prophet, just as Isaiah, Jeremiah, and Ezekiel employed acted parables in communicating their messages. This particular interpretation is also consistent with the overall program of the Messiah-King for the Jerusalem temple, which we know from the Scriptures, and Jesus himself predicts, such as in Matt 24:2. It is equally consistent with the nature, calling, and intentions of the Messiah-King to interpret the temple incident as Jesus' protest against the apparent commercialization of the temple institution and against the ruling priests' apparent failure in the discharge of their spiritual duties over the people.

The temple incident would have been relevant in specific ways to the Matthean community. The Matthean emphasis on Jesus as the Davidic Messiah, highlighted very clearly in Matthew's account of Jesus' temple act, would have been both a timely theological education and a much-needed boost of morale for the predominantly Jewish-Christian community as they might have faced interrogations and hostilities emanating from the surrounding Jewish and non-Christian social environments. One accusation that might have been leveled against these Jewish Christians was that they were so foolish and gullible to have exchanged the religion of Abraham (Judaism) with a cultic heresy (Christianity). Another accusation, perhaps coming from their loved ones, might have to do with betrayal—these Jewish Christians betrayed not only their ancestral religion but also the trust of their loved ones and friends. But no; they were not gullible, and they did not exchange their ancestral religion for a heresy. In fact, Jesus is the Davidic Messiah that they as Jews had been waiting for all along. In this sense, they actually did not betray their ancestral religion. Jesus in fact was and is the full manifestation of Yahweh. He is the Immanuel, as Matthew tells in the early part of his Gospel. We are not certain how deeply the Matthean community understood or grasped this nuanced Christology, but we can be sure that Matthew's Gospel presented to them a Jesus who fulfilled the law and the prophets, a Jesus who is the anticipated Davidic Messiah, and that being so, they might have posed the question: "What remains of the Jewish Law? What remains of the Jewish temple?" When they read Matthew's account of Jesus' temple act, they might not have fully grasped Matthew's intentions, but at least they would have probably been convinced that Jesus is the real deal.

3

The Significance of the Marcan Temple Incident

CONTEXTUAL CONSIDERATIONS[1]

OUR PURPOSE IN THIS chapter is to determine the significance of the Marcan temple incident (11:15–19) by the use of a compositional analysis. As did chapter 2, this chapter will proceed in three movements. The first will seek to grasp the big picture of Mark. What is this book all about? Who wrote it? When? Where? Who were the recipients? Why was it written? What was the probable life setting of its original readers? What are its themes and key emphases?

Secondly, we will consider the immediate contexts of the Marcan temple incident, namely Jesus' entry into Jerusalem (11:1–11) and the cursing of the fig tree and the tree's consequent withering (11:12–14, 20–26). We will then analyze the temple incident itself. We will examine its language, determine its structure, and identify its key themes and emphases. Then, for the third and final movement, we will step back and inquire how the overall message, key themes and emphases of this pericope relate to and cohere with Mark's overall message, emphases, and purposes. Then we will

---

1. Refer to Appendix 1 for a comparison of the contextual location of Jesus' temple act in the Gospels.

be able to state or express the meaning or significance of Jesus' temple act in Mark.

Mark's Overall Message and Emphases

The second Gospel has come to be known as the Gospel of Mark. That attribution was not originally there, as was the case with the other Gospels. The earliest evidence we have that explicitly supports Marcan authorship of the second Gospel is that of Papias (ca. 60-130 CE), who served as bishop of Hierapolis in Phrygia of Asia Minor. Church historian Eusebius preserves Papias's testimony for us in *Hist. eccl.* (AD 325).

> But now we must add to the words of [Papias'] which we have already quoted the tradition which he gives in regard to Mark, the author of the Gospel. It is in the following words: "This also John the Presbyter said: Mark, having become the interpreter of Peter, wrote down accurately, though not indeed in order, whatever he remembered of the things said or done by Christ. For he neither heard the Lord nor accompanied him, but afterward, as I said, he was in company with Peter, who used to offer teaching as necessity demanded, but with no intention of giving a connected account of the Lord's discourses. So Mark committed no error in thus writing some single points, as he remembered them. For upon one thing he fixed his attention: to leave nothing of what he had heard and to make no false statements in them." (3.39.15)[2]

This testimony affirms the following: (1) Mark wrote the second Gospel; (2) Mark's source of information was the apostle Peter, having become the latter's interpreter; (3) Mark wrote the second Gospel "accurately, though not indeed in order"; and (4) Mark made no mistake in writing his Gospel.

Marcan authorship[3] was also supported by many other ancient Christian writers including Justin Martyr, *Dial.* 106; Irenaeus, *Haer.* 3.1.2;

2. *NPNF*[2] 1:172-3.

3. Contemporary scholars who accept Papias's testimony include, among others, Yarbrough, "Date of Papias"; Gundry, *Mark*, 1026-34; France, *Gospel of Mark*, 7-8, 37-41; Brooks, *Mark*, 25-27; Keener, *Background*, 132; Köstenberger, Kellum, and Quarles, *Cradle*, 231-32; Hengel, *Studies*, 47-50; Cranfield, *Gospel*, 5. Some other scholars, such as Kümmel (*Introduction*, 97), Achtemeier ("Mark"), and Telford (*Mark*, 15-20) argue that we cannot establish the identity of the second Gospel's author on the basis of Papias's testimony. Achtemeier, for example, thinks that Papias "ought not to be taken at face value" (p. 542). For a summary of arguments marshaled against Papias and a response to these arguments, see Gundry, *Mark*, 1038-45. So these scholars abandon what Telford

Tertullian, *Marc.* 4.5; Clement of Alexandria, *Hyp.* (according to Eusebius, *Hist. eccl.* 6.14.5–7); Origen, *Comm. Matt.* (again according to Eusebius, *Hist. eccl.* 6.25.5); and, probably, the Muratorian Canon.[4] Considering all of these testimonies, Brooks wrote: "The early church was unanimous that Mark was the author of the Gospel."[5] Lane speaks of "an unbroken tradition" putting forth "John Mark" as the Gospel's author.[6] Keener points out that "because there is no evidence against this attribution, Mark is the most likely candidate for the author."[7]

Who is this Mark whom Papias credited with writing the second Gospel? Do we have good reasons for supposing that this Mark is the same John Mark mentioned in Acts (2:12, 25; 13:5, 13; 15:37) and in four epistles (Col 4:10; Phlm 24; 2 Tim 4:11; 1 Pet 5:13)? Conservative scholars think so. For example, Lane wrote his commentary on the assumption that this Mark and John Mark were the same person.[8] Carson and Moo are equally certain.[9] They argue that external evidence—that is, the church fathers' testimonies—overwhelmingly favors the authorship of John Mark. In terms of internal evidence, they cite two factors as supporting John Mark as the author. First, "the Greek style of Mark's Gospel is simple and straightforward and full of the kind of Semitisms that one would expect of a Jerusalem-bred Christian." Second, "Mark's connection with Paul may help explain what many scholars have found to be a Pauline theological influence in the second gospel." They conclude: "Nothing in the second gospel stands in the way of accepting the earliest tradition that identifies John Mark as its author."[10]

The main reason for the rejection by certain critical scholars of the Papias tradition concerning the second Gospel is that they do not accept Papias's explanation for the origins of the Gospel. For Papias, writing the second Gospel involved only three stages: it all began with Jesus—his words

---

calls a "fruitless search for the named individual responsible for the text and instead to construct a more general profile of the historical author in terms of his (or her) cultural background, socio-political situation and religious concerns" (*Mark*, 15).

4. Carson and Moo, *Introduction*, 173. For an extensive study of how ancient Christian writers viewed the authorship of Mark, see Oden and Hall, *Mark*, xxi–xxxv.

5. Brooks, *Mark*, 26.

6. Lane, *Gospel*, 21.

7. Keener, *Background*, 132.

8. See especially Lane's discussion of authorship in *Gospel*, 21–23.

9. Carson and Moo, *Introduction*, 173–74.

10. Carson and Moo, *Introduction*, 174.

The Significance of the Marcan Temple Incident

and deeds; then, there was the apostolic mediation—Peter's recollections; and then finally, there was Mark who wrote the final product—the second Gospel. Those who reject this short, clean-cut explanation argue, however, that the Marcan material went through several stages of development. Gundry explains this position thus:

> The needs of church life and evangelism shaped the materials; and the supernatural elements in stories such as those of Jesus' baptism, raising of Jairus's daughter, transfiguration, and resurrection, etc., are too fantastic to have come from someone so close to what really happened as Peter was. The narrative of Jesus' long delay in Capernaum arises out of *artistic manipulation* of originally *unrelated traditions*, not out of the actuality of concatenated events as narrated by someone who was there; and Mark drew on earlier collections of controversy stories, miracle stories, sayings, parables, and on an earlier passion narrative.[11]

The bone of contention is historicity. Does Mark reflect actual history or not? Papias's account says yes, while skeptical scholarship, starting with William Wrede, says no. Wrede popularized the theory of the "messianic secret," which was his interpretive schema of the second Gospel. He argued that Mark contains an *evolved* theology of its author that was further based upon the theology of the early church. Explaining Wrede's well-known "messianic secret," Moritz writes,

> Historically, Wrede argued, Jesus did not regard himself as Messiah. The disciples' alleged lack of understanding and Jesus' reported enjoinders to keep his messianic role and status secret . . . supposedly were introduced into the pre-Markan tradition to explain why Jesus' messiahship only came about as a consequence of the resurrection kerygma.[12]

Mark's reports of Jesus forbidding his followers from telling forth his miraculous deeds proved to be a stumbling block for Wrede and his followers. Culpepper points out that "most conservative New Testament scholars now argue that Wrede forced a false dichotomy between the mind of Jesus and the mind of Mark."[13] While it is true that Mark is a theological work, it is possible to posit that Mark's Christology "goes back to the earliest levels and even to Jesus himself. Marcan secrecy (which many would judge that

11. Gundry, *Mark*, 1038.
12. Moritz, "Mark," 480; see also Schröter, "Gospel," 272.
13. Culpepper, *Mark*, 9.

Wrede exaggerated) may have its roots in Jesus' historical rejection of some messianic aspirations of his own time."[14] Additionally, Culpepper wrote,

> The emphasis on secrecy probably originated with Jesus rather than with Mark. Jesus may well have commanded secrecy to avoid the misunderstanding that he was merely a wonder worker and to discourage further suspicion from the religious and political authorities. After all, secrecy was inherent in the nature of his mission—God in the form of a servant.[15]

The question of when Mark's Gospel was written is closely allied to that of why it was written. This has far-reaching implications for our understanding and interpretation of the Marcan text. Proposed dates can be generally grouped into three: (1) pre-65 CE, (2) 65–75 CE, and (3) post-75 CE. The 65–75 CE range is supported by majority of scholars of different theological persuasions.[16] Scholars supporting the pre-65 CE date have proposed varying dates ranging from the 40s to the mid 60s. Scholars supporting the post-75 CE dating have proposed varying dates ranging from early 75 to the second century CE. According to Crossley, "the earlier dates have gained more respectability, even if the vast majority of scholars do not accept them, and are advocated largely, but not exclusively, by conservative scholars."[17]

The early church writings, which serve as our external clues to dating Mark, unanimously support a pre-70 CE date. These early testimonies, however, are divided when we use Peter's death, 64/65 CE (see *1 Clem.* 5), as the demarcation date. The *Anti-Marcionite Prologue* and Irenaeus (185 CE; see *Haer.* 3.1.1) date Mark after Peter's death. A possible additional support for this, according to Carson and Moo,[18] is Papias's citation of the presbyter: "Mark, who had been Peter's interpreter" (Eusebius, *Hist. eccl.*

---

14. Brown, *Introduction*, 153.

15. Culpepper, *Mark*, 9.

16. So Crossley, *Date*, 1. Proponents include Taylor, *Gospel*, 31–32; Cranfield, *Gospel*, 8; Brandon, "Date"; Kelber, *Kingdom*; Kümmel, *Introduction*, 97–98; Bruce, "Date"; Hengel, *Studies*, 1–28; Radcliffe, "Son of Man"; Senior, "Setting"; Mack, *Myth*; Myers, *Binding*; Guelich, *Mark 1–8*, xxxi–xxxvii; Sanders and Davies, *Synoptic Gospels*, 5–21; Hooker, *Commentary*, 8; Marcus, "War"; Marcus, *Mark 1–8*, 37–39; Theissen, *Gospels*, 258–71; Van Iersel, "Followers"; Telford, *Theology*, 12–13; Witherington, *Gospel*, 30–31.

17. Crossley, *Date*, 2. So, for example, Harnack, *Date*; Allen, *Gospel*; Torrey, *Documents*, 1–40; Robinson, *Redating*, 106–17; Wenham, *Redating*, 136–82, 238; Ellis, "Date"; Thiede, *Manuscript*; Casey, *Sources*, 259–60.

18. Carson and Moo, *Introduction*, 181.

3.39.15; note the verb tense). Justin Martyr (*Dial.* 106.3) may also be further cited in support of this position.[19]

In contrast to this, Clement of Alexandria (Eusebius, *Hist. eccl.* 6.14.6-7) and Origen (Eusebius, *Hist. eccl.* 6.25.5) date Mark before Peter's death (before 64/65 CE). Trying to reconcile these two conflicting traditions was probably the reason why some scholars[20] posit that Mark began writing his Gospel during Peter's lifetime but finished and published it after his death.[21] The weight of external evidence, however, clearly tilts in favor of a date after Peter's death considering that our earliest testimony, the *Anti-Marcionite Prologue* (ca. 160 CE), supports it. Additionally, Peter's death can be viewed as the proximate cause for Mark's writing the Gospel.

A number of internal evidence has been identified in support of the late 60s dating. Carson and Moo cite two.[22] First is Mark's emphasis on Jesus' disciples following "the 'road to the cross' walked by our Lord. This emphasis best fits a situation when Christians were facing the grim prospect of martyrdom, a setting that would have obtained in Rome at the time of, or after, Nero's famous persecution of Christians in AD 65." Second, Mark 13 reflects "the situation in Palestine during the Jewish revolt and just before the Roman entrance into the city," and thus Mark may be confidently dated between 67 and 69.

But this evidence is not without difficulties. Both Marcus[23] and Stein[24] have mounted strong disagreement over using the Marcan emphasis on suffering and Mark 13 as basis for establishing a date. Stein has a different explanation for Mark's warning about suffering: "Acts reveals that from the beginning the church experienced persecution and most of Paul's warnings concerning Christian persecution were written before AD 64/65." On Mark 13, Stein writes, "The exhortation to flee Jerusalem is not addressed to Mark's readers, who probably reside in either Rome or Syria but certainly not in Judea . . . Hence it does not serve the purpose of dating the Gospel."[25]

---

19. Stein, *Mark*, 13.
20. Zahn (*Introduction*, 2:433-34) and Guthrie (*Introduction*, 86) seem favorable to it.
21. Carson and Moo, *Introduction*, 181 n. 40.
22. Carson and Moo, *Introduction*, 181.
23. Marcus, *Mark 1-8*, 32-33.
24. Stein, *Mark*, 14-15.
25. Stein, *Mark*, 14.

The Significance of the Temple Incident in the Narratives of the Four Gospels

The internal evidence does not really help to pinpoint a narrow dating for Mark. The external evidence is much clearer. Combining them, two conclusions are reached and upheld in this book. First, Mark was probably written prior to 70 CE. The implication of that of course on our reading of Mark 13 and the rest of the Gospel is clear. Mark 13 is prophecy, not a recounting of history. As Guelich has pointed out, the context of Mark 13 is Jesus' prediction of the destruction of the temple (13:1–2), which was his answer to the disciples' query about when "these things" would take place.[26] Second, evidence compels us to be generous and broadminded in deciding which pre-70 CE date we assign for Mark's writing. It is hard to be dogmatic here. Carson and Moo's proposal is enough to serve our pesent purposes: "sometime in the late 50s or the 60s."[27]

In terms of Mark's provenance (where the Gospel was written), three places have been proposed: Rome, Syria, and Galilee.[28] Early tradition favors Rome. For example, the *Anti-Marcionite Prologue* claims that Mark wrote his Gospel account "in the regions of Italy," which is supported by both Irenaeus (*Haer.* 3.1.2) and Clement of Alexandria (as per Eusebius, *Hist. eccl.* 6.14.6–7). The following factors are said to support Roman provenance: (1) the large number of Latinisms in Mark;[29] (2) the incidental mention of Simon of Cyrene's sons, Alexander and Rufus, at least one of whom may have been known to Mark in Rome (in Romans 16:13, the apostle Paul greets Rufus); (3) the apparently Gentile audience of the Gospel; (4) the many allusions to suffering, which would be appropriate if the Gospel was written under the shadow of persecutions of the church in Rome; (5) the fact that 1 Pet 5:13 locates Mark in Rome with Peter in the early 60s; and (6) the connection with an important early center of Christianity, which would have explained the Gospel's quick acceptance.[30]

If Mark was written in Rome and if we for the sake of argument limit its date to late 60s, then we can reconstruct the situation that might have called for its writing. We do have a number of indications from the early church that Mark was written primarily for Christians in Rome (and Italy). The imperial ruler during this time was Nero. In the early 60s the situation

---

26. Guelich, *Mark 1–8*, xxxi.

27. Carson and Moo, *Introduction*, 182.

28. See Winn, *Purpose*, 76–91; Culpepper, *Mark*, 25–29. They both support Roman provenance.

29. See Winn, *Purpose*, 80–82.

30. See Carson and Moo, *Introduction*, 177, for more discussion.

in Rome was not yet bad for Christians. But the fateful burning of the imperial capital in 64 CE not only destroyed the physical makeup of Rome but also became the impetus that kicked off the massive Neronian persecution of Christians.[31] Lane writes,

> On this understanding, Mark's task was the projection of Christian faith in a context of suffering and martyrdom. If Christians were to be strengthened and the gospel effectively proclaimed it would be necessary to exhibit the similarity of situation faced by Jesus and the Christians of Rome. The Gospel of Mark is a pastoral response to this critical demand.[32]

However, this reconstruction, though supported by many scholars, is by no means free of difficulties. At best it is a tentative one. Our conclusion on Mark's purpose must therefore be guided by and based on textual clues.

Scholars have subjected Mark to virtually all sorts of known methodologies: redaction criticism, reader-response criticism, forms of structuralism, narrative criticism, socio-rhetorical criticism, socio-political criticism, and so forth.[33] This bewildering array of varying approaches and conclusions can potentially confuse the basic question with which we are concerned: what is Mark's chief concern or message in writing his Gospel? We must turn to the text itself, reading it several times, analyzing the narrative flow, the selection and arrangement of material, editorial comments, recurring themes, and the like.

On close reading of the text, we will see that Mark is characterized by the following. First, there is a focus on Jesus' activity, especially his performance of miracles. Second, there is a focus on Jesus' passion (suffering). It is as Martin Kähler commented: Mark is "a passion narrative with an extended introduction."[34] Third, there is repeated correlation of Jesus' predicted sufferings and the "cost of discipleship."

These three prominent foci are pointers to the key themes of the Gospel. First, there is the theme of Christology. In fact, the whole of the Gospel's narrative is mainly about Jesus of Nazareth.[35] The Gospel opens with

---

31. See Lane, *Gospel*, 13–14, and his footnoted literature there for a description of the scale of this persecution.
32. Lane, *Gospel*, 15.
33. Brown, *Introduction*, 152.
34. Quoted in Carson and Moo, *Introduction*, 185.
35. Donahue and Harrington, *Gospel*, 23. Schnelle (*Theology*, 405) writes: "As theology proper is the foundation of Markan thought, so Christology is its center."

the following words: "The beginning of the good news of Jesus Christ, the Son of God" (1:1). By focusing on Jesus' miracles and passion, Mark thus presents a wholesome and balanced Christology—a Christ of both power and suffering, of both glory and humility.[36] But again it is worth noting that Mark's presentation of Christology is narrative, not didactic and systematic.

The second theme is discipleship. If Mark's main figure is Jesus, he presents Jesus in relation to his disciples.[37] This becomes apparent when we examine the Gospel's structure and content. Donahue and Harrington note that every major section of the Gospel begins with a discipleship pericope.[38] They further note the following: the disciples' mission parallels that of Jesus (3:13–19; 6:7–13); they are recipients of Jesus' private instruction (4:10–34; 7:1–23; the bulk of 8:27—10:45 is devoted to discipleship; 13:1–37); the disciples are privileged witnesses to Jesus' deeds (4:35–41; 5:37–43; 6:45–52; 9:2–8); they assist him in feeding the multitudes (6:30–44; 8:1–10) and share a meal with him (14:12–26); Jesus promises to go before them into Galilee (14:28); and finally, the women are told to inform the disciples that Jesus will meet them in Galilee (16:7).

Another aspect of the theme of discipleship in Mark is that the disciples' call/commissioning becomes a paradigm of discipleship (1:16–20; 3:13–19; 6:6b–13) for future believers. Donahue and Harrington identify several stages to this call/commissioning based on 1:16–20, which are repeated in subsequent records in Mark: (1) Jesus initiates the call; (2) those called are engaged in day-to-day work; (3) the call is in the form of clear summons ("follow me"); (4) the essence of the call is to share in Jesus' mission; (5) the response to the call is immediate, spontaneous ("unreflective"), and there is a leaving of former occupations; and finally (6) responding to

---

36. Gundry (*Mark*) is right in observing that Mark poses a literary problem by presenting two kinds of disparate material: one dealing with Jesus' successes "which make him look like others admired in the Greco-Roman world for their divine powers of wisdom, clairvoyance, exorcism, thaumaturgy, and personal magnetism," and second dealing with Jesus' suffering and persecution. "The basic problem in Marcan studies is how to fit these apparently contradictory kinds of material in a way that makes sense of the book as a literary whole" (p. 2).

37. For France (*Gospel of Mark*, 28), Mark's christological message and focus does not mean that discipleship is out of the picture. He explains that it is the disciples' discovery of and response to who Jesus is that they occupy our attention; "discipleship is the proper outcome of a healthy Christology."

38. Donahue and Harrington, *Gospel*, 30. See their outline on 47–50.

the call is not private but an entrance into a community of those who have responded to the same call.[39]

A final note of discipleship in Mark is reflected in 8:34, "If any want to become my followers, let them deny themselves and take up their cross and follow me." For Mark, being Jesus' disciple means walking the way he walked—the road of selflessness, of suffering, which is in fact the true road to glory.

Besides Christology and discipleship, there are other themes that are pointed out in Mark. Some of the significant ones are kingdom of God and eschatology.[40]

In the light of Mark's key themes—in particular, Christology and discipleship—and on the assumption that Mark was written to believers in Rome during the massive Neronian persecution of Christians in the mid-60s, we can reasonably approximate on Mark's purposes as follows. First, he intended his readers to realize and learn that this Jesus whom they have believed in was not only the miracle-working Christ but also the suffering Son of God. Second (and logically flowing from the first), disciples of Jesus are to walk in the same way—the way of selfless suffering, cross-bearing, which may sometimes entail losing one's life. Jesus himself bore the cross and lost his life not for himself but for humanity. Mark summarizes this in a way that nails the point: "If any want to become my followers, let them deny themselves and take up their cross and follow me" (8:34).

There have been three significant monographs that have approached Mark using a single theme or scheme of interpretation. First is Joel Marcus's *The Way of the Lord* (1992). Marcus analyzed the Markan Gospel by (1) locating those passages in the Gospel where the evangelist has referred to the OT, (2) investigating into how he used those sources, (3) deconstructing the Markan form to find out his redaction of the sources, and (4) investigating the early Jewish and Christian interpretations of those OT passages used by Mark. The outcome is that, for Marcus, Mark has constructed a worldview of messianic fulfillment that is essentially distinct from the Jewish Zealot ideology, which had come to nothing with the fall of Jerusalem in 70 CE.

The second book is R. H. Gundry's *Mark: A Commentary on His Apology for the Cross* (1993). Gundry's understanding of why Mark wrote his Gospel is indicated in the subtitle. Mark is "a straightforward apology

---

39. Donahue and Harrington, *Gospel*, 31.

40. Schnelle, *Theology*, 402–3; Donahue and Harrington, *Gospel*, 307–8; France, *Gospel of Mark*, 29–33.

[read: defense] for the Cross, for the shameful way in which the object of Christian faith and subject of Christian proclamation died, and hence for Jesus as the Crucified One."[41] Though the cross symbolized curse, suffering, and shame, this apology is now possible because, as Mark's Gospel ends not with the cross but the empty tomb, God has vindicated the Messiah by raising him up from the dead; hence, quoting another NT writer, "God has made him both Lord and Christ—this Jesus whom you crucified" (Acts 2:22–24, 36).

Gundry's proposal—in spite of its merits—has two basic weaknesses. First, as implied in the title, Gundry would like us to believe that Mark was meant for non-Christians, but that is quite doubtful in consideration of both the internal and external evidence (see discussion above). Second, it is equally doubtful whether this one-purpose scheme will be able to do full justice to the complex narrative of the Gospel.

The third book is R. E. Watts's *Isaiah's New Exodus and Mark* (1997).[42] Watts himself acknowledged that his study was influenced by Joel Marcus's 1992 book. The difference is that whereas Marcus generally surveyed OT texts that Mark used in his Gospel, Watts specifically focused on Isaianic passages referenced in Mark. Watts begins by noting the frequency of Mark's references to the Exodus motifs such as the wilderness (in Mark's prologue), the feeding stories, and the transfiguration episode (cloud dwellings), with its reference to Moses and the sea crossings. He combines it then with Mark's editorial combination of Isa 40:3 with Mal 3:1 and Exod 23:20 in Mark's opening verses. What emerges from this "is an important hermeneutical key to this Gospel."[43] Apparently, Watts's hermeneutical scheme is a successful one, as evidenced by the international acclaim that his book has generated.

Mark's overall narrative seems to have two general sections, 1:1—8:26 and 8:27—16:8.[44] It is remarkable that this division seems to equally halve the Gospel. Each part is of course very long and broad and can be subdivided. These two parts are equivalent to what Gundry calls "two disparate kinds of material." The first describes Jesus' successes—"Jesus attracts disciples, draws crowds, exorcises demons, works miracles, teaches with

---

41. Gundry, *Gospel*, 1.

42. Watts's scheme has found an avid following in T. Moritz ("Mark").

43. Moritz, "Mark," 481. For a summary of how Watts's scheme applies to the interpretation of Mark, see Moritz, "Mark," 481–84.

44. Brown, *Introduction*, 126–48.

authority, [and] bests his opponents in debates." The second portrays Jesus as "a persecuted one." "He predicts his passion. One of his closest disciples betrays him. The rest forsake him. The leading one of the rest denies him. The Jewish authorities condemn him. The crowd yell for his crucifixion."[45]

However, viewed geographically, Mark's narrative will militate against the said two-part outline. Geographically, therefore, Mark's narrative seems to call for a three-point outline:[46] (1) 1:1—8:21, Jesus ministers in Galilee; (2) 8:22—10:52, Jesus journeys to Jerusalem; and (3) 11:1—16:8, Jesus in Jerusalem, his suffering, death, and resurrection.

The Immediate Context

As in Matthew and Luke, but not in John, Jesus' dramatic entry into Jerusalem in Mark's Gospel serves as a background for the temple incident. But in distinction from the other Synoptic Gospels, in Mark the temple incident does not happen on the day of Jesus' entry into Jerusalem but on the following day. Also in Mark the temple incident is sandwiched between Jesus' cursing the fig tree and the fig tree's withering. The entry into the city, the action in the temple, and the cursing of the fig tree are all dramatic acts of Jesus, and their grouping together in Mark's narrative indicates their thematic and semantic interrelatedness and similarity.

Below we will examine Jesus' entry into Jerusalem and his cursing of the fig tree and inquire how these dramatic acts shed light on our understanding of Jesus' equally dramatic action in the temple. We will also inquire how Mark's distinct timing—the one-day interval between Jesus' entry to Jerusalem and the action in the temple—affects the meaning that Mark wanted to invest into the temple action.

Jesus' Entry into Jerusalem (11:1–11)

In Mark's narratival scheme, this is the first time that Jesus goes into Jerusalem. This is of course artificial and purely literary for there are hints that Jesus had been to Jerusalem several times before. Mark himself hints at this in 14:3 where Jesus was apparently known to Simon the leper. The evangelist John mentions two other visits, and Matt 23:37 (par. Luke 13:34)

---

45. Gundry, *Mark*, 2.
46. Such as advocated by France, *Gospel of Mark*, 13–14.

also implies other visits. Mark's scheme thus heightens the dramatic nature of Jesus' entry to Jerusalem.

We also need to remind ourselves of what Jerusalem stood for in relation to Jesus. Van Iersel correctly observes that by entering into Jerusalem, Jesus enters "the lion's den."[47] From the beginning, he knew his mission and destiny, and he spoke plainly about this to his disciples, saying that "the Son of Man must undergo great suffering, and be rejected by the elders, the chief priests, and the scribes, and be killed, and after three days rise again" (8:31–32). By mentioning the elders, chief priests and teachers of the law, Jesus seems to be pointing to the Sanhedrin whose seat of power was in Jerusalem. In Mark 10:32–34, Jesus directly mentioned Jerusalem to his disciples, again predicting his death. That he was a Galilean and a foreigner in Jerusalem was not the issue that brought him in conflict with the Jewish authorities. He is the "Son of Man" (Mark 8:31; 10:33), the "Son of David" (Mark 10:47), and the heir to the "kingdom of David" (Mark 11:10); in other words, the expected Messiah, the King of Israel, and his entry into Jerusalem dramatizes that identity.

The title "Son of Man," which Jesus applied to himself in Mark 8:31 and 10:33, has its roots in prophet Daniel's "one like a son of man" (7:13–14) and this prophetic passage was understood by many Jewish interpreters during Jesus' time as referring to the Messiah.[48] Scholars of various stripes acknowledge that "there existed in pre-Christian apocalyptic Judaism a concept of the eschatological Son of Man, a transcendent and pre-existent being . . ."[49]

As for the title "Son of David," it is very interesting that the blind Bartimaeus has applied it twice to Jesus (10:47, 48). As a Jew living in the first century, Bartimaeus might have shared with his fellow Jews the expectation of a coming king from the lineage of David. E. J. Prins explains, "In the period between 200 BC and 100 AD, there are Jewish communities that applied biblical texts about a messiah to a bringer of salvation in the end times who would establish a kingdom of peace. This royal bringer of salvation was called 'the Messiah.'"[50] As for Bartimaeus, Jesus is the Son of David,

---

47. Van Iersel, *Mark*, 350.

48. Burkett, *Son of Man*, 23.

49. Higgins, *Son of Man*, 3. To name some, Tödt, *Son of Man*, ch. 1; Hahn, *Titles*, ch. 1; Fuller, *Foundations*, 34–43; Barrett, *Jesus*, 32; Conzelmann, *Outline*, 131–37; Teeple, "ὁ υἱός τοῦ ἀνθρώπου"; Borsch, *Son of Man*.

50. Prins, *Messiah*, 14.

who possesses healing powers.[51] It is quite instructive that Jesus did not silence or discourage Bartimaeus from calling him the Son of David. He accepted that designation, and he restored Bartimaeus's sight.

One final introductory note is that Jesus' entry into Jerusalem serves both as the culmination of his and his band's long journey from Galilee to Jerusalem, starting from Mark 8:21 to 10:52, and as the beginning of Jesus' last public presence and ministry in the capital, leading eventually to his passion, crucifixion, and resurrection.

Preparations for the Entry (vv. 1–6)

It is significant to note where the preparation for the Jerusalem entry takes place: outside the city of Jerusalem, at Bethany and Bethphage in the slope of the Mount of Olives. Bethany is a significant place for it will serve as Jesus' home base during the passion week (Mark 11:11–12; 14:3–9). Donahue and Harrington are of the opinion that Jesus and his band arrived at Bethany, and the town where Jesus sends his two disciples to fetch a colt is Bethphage.[52] That is of course a good possibility.[53] Keeping it clear in mind that the events of Mark 11:1–10 did not take place in the capital will spare us from wrongly equating the crowd who acclaimed Jesus (these were fellow pilgrims with Jesus) with the crowd who called for his execution (these were mainly Judean and Jerusalem Jews).[54]

Jesus, accompanied by his twelve disciples and the pilgrim crowd, has been approaching Jerusalem on foot. However, at this point in the journey, when they are only a few kilometers to their destination, Jesus stops and makes arrangement for his entry into Jerusalem on a colt. He sends two disciples to fetch a colt, and he specifies that it is a colt "which no one has ever ridden" (11:2; cf. Luke 19:30). The two disciples are to untie it and bring it to Jesus. If anyone confronts them for untying the colt, they are to

---

51. For a survey of the origins and development of the concept of a messiah from the Davidic line, see H. Schwarz, *Eschatology*, 49–51. For a helpful study of the origins of the concept of a "therapeutic" Son of David and related themes, see L. Novakovic, *Messiah*, 78–79.

52. Donahue and Harrington, *Gospel*, 321.

53. Lane (*Gospel*, 395) and Van Iersel (*Mark*, 352) favor this suggestion; Gundry (*Gundry*, 624) argues the opposite.

54. Hence the flawed argument that the crowd was being fickle, one time acclaiming Jesus and another time wishing him to die.

say, "The Lord needs it and will send it back here shortly" (11:3).⁵⁵ Jesus' order is carried out exactly (11:4-6). Verse 7 says that the disciples bring the colt to Jesus, they put their garments on it, and Jesus sits on it.

Jesus' Entry to Jerusalem (vv. 8-10)

The pilgrim crowd who have been with Jesus (as Jesus himself is a pilgrim like them) appear in the scene very actively in verses 8-10. The πολλοὶ ("many people") and ἄλλοι ("others") of verse 8 indicate the big size of the crowd. They spread on the road their τὰ ἱμάτια ("cloaks," "clothes") and the στιβάδας ("straws") that they have cut from the fields. Στιβάς differs from John's τὰ βαΐα τῶν φοινίκων ("palm branches"). It refers generally to vegetation, including "straw, rushes, leaves, and other materials used for bedding."⁵⁶ Stein translates it as "leafy branches or tall blades of grass."⁵⁷

There is more action by the crowd in verses 9 and 10. Mark's narrative puts Jesus in between two groups of people altogether comprising the crowd. Those ahead of Jesus and those following him shout,

A Ὡσαννά

  B Εὐλογημένος ὁ ἐρχόμενος ἐν ὀνόματι κυρίου

  B Εὐλογημένη ἡ ἐρχομένη βασιλεία τοῦ πατρὸς ἡμῶν Δαυίδ

A Ὡσαννά ἐν τοῖς ὑψίστοις.⁵⁸

Ὡσαννά ("Save us now") comes from Ps 118:25. Εὐλογημένος ὁ ἐρχόμενος ἐν ὀνόματι κυρίου ("Blessed is he who comes in the name of the Lord")

---

55. Ὁ κύριος in Mark 11:3 and parallels have generated discussions. Does it refer to God, to Jesus, or to the human owner of the colt? France (*Gospel of Mark*, 433) argues that it refers to God: the colt is needed for God's service which enhances Jesus' claim for the significance of his own arrival in Jerusalem. Gundry (*Mark*, 624), following J. D. M. Derrett (*Law*, 241-58), argues that it refers to Jesus who exercised "a lordly prerogative by requisitioning the colt as a means of transportation." R. G. Bratcher ("Note," 93) argues that Jesus was the real owner of the colt, for he acquired it in preparation for his coming. Lane (*Gospel*, 395) argues that Jesus' "precise knowledge concerning the animal and its availability suggests prearrangement with the owner, who may have been with Jesus at the time." Because of the ambiguity, Van Iesel (*Mark*, 352-53) thinks that perhaps Mark might have been playing on the three possible meanings of "the Lord."

56. France, *Gospel of Mark*, 433.

57. Stein, *Mark*, 505.

58. I owe this chiastic structure to France, *Gospel of Mark*, 433; see also Lane, *Gospel*, 397.

comes from Ps 118:26a. Psalms 113–118 are known as the Hallel Psalms, and they "were used liturgically in connection with Passover and Tabernacles, serving as a focus for prayer, praise and thanksgiving for every pious Jew."[59] The original usage and function of "Hosanna" was a prayer for God's saving action. But this function disappeared in the first century and the word became "an expression of joy and jubilation."[60] The original function of the clause "blessed is he who comes in the name of the Lord" might have been as a welcoming greeting of the priests addressed to a worshiper coming into the temple. So it is not necessarily messianic.

The crowd's chant continues in Mark 11:10, but this time the words do not come from Ps 118. Three words from Mark 11:9 are repeated, with a change from masculine ("Εὐλογημένος ὁ ἐρχόμενος . . .") to feminine gender ("Εὐλογημένη ἡ ἐρχομένη . . .") due of course to a change of subject: in verse 9, "the coming one" (or "he" [who comes]); in verse 10, "the kingdom" (ἡ βασιλεία). Hooker suggests that this parallel (Εὐλογημένος ὁ ἐρχόμενος . . . Εὐλογημένη ἡ ἐρχομένη . . .) confirms "that the one who is welcomed also brings the kingdom."[61] Hence, Mark 11:10 has both royal and messianic connotations.

In Jerusalem (v. 11)

What is remarkable is the brevity of Mark's description of what happens when Jesus is in the city (v. 11) in contrast to the lengthy description he devotes to describing Jesus' approach to the city (vv. 1–10). As Van Iersel observes, "The story fizzles out"[62] and unexpectedly Mark pictures Jesus acting alone: note, for instance, the repetition of "he" in verse 11. What happens to the crowd? How does the city (whether officials or common people) react to Jesus' entry?[63] Apparently Mark's focus was not on these details. It is precisely because of the absence of these details that the few things he records stand out very conspicuously. Jesus, here pictured alone, enters the city, goes to the temple, and inspects everything there. The word used for temple is ἱερόν (also in 11:15, 16, 27; 12:35; 13:2; and 14:49) which

---

59. Lane, *Gospel*, 397.
60. Stein, *Mark*, 505; cf. Hooker, *Commentary*, 260; Fitzmyer, "Aramaic Evidence."
61. Hooker, *Commentary*, 259–60.
62. Van Iersel, *Mark*, 354.
63. Matthew tells us that the whole city was stirred and asked, "Who Is This?" (21:10).

refers to the "whole collection of places and buildings inside the sacred area of the Temple terrace . . . it often denotes the outer courts accessible to pagans, with the porticos (the Royal Portico on the southern boundary, with its three hundred and sixty columns and its three aisles; Solomon's Porch stretching along the eastern boundary and dominating the Valley of Cedron)."[64] Jesus looked at the temple in the sense of inspecting what was going on in there, but Mark does not tell us what Jesus sees in there or his reaction to what he sees. But we do know that Jesus has been to the temple many times before (as the evangelist John indicates), so he does not inspect the temple as a curious tourist. It is unlikely that Jesus had only formed his judgment on the redundancy of the temple system during this instance of inspection. The fact that Mark tells us only of Jesus' inspection of the temple implies that for Mark this event is very consequential for what will eventually transpire in his narrative. Similarly, Gray is of the opinion that verse 11 is "a pregnant pause giving time for the narrative tension and the reader's anticipation to build as the conflict between Jesus and the temple establishment draws near."[65]

Key Themes Emanating from Mark's Account of Jesus' Entry to Jerusalem

Fresh from our textual analysis of Mark's account of the entry, we are now ready to identify the themes that Mark has sought to foreground. We can expect that Mark has themes shared with the other Gospels. But overall, we will be able to see Mark's distinct emphases for his account of the entry, and this will in turn assist our analysis and understanding of the temple incident.

The Theme of Royalty (Kingship)

Mark's account of the entry contains certain elements that clearly portray Jesus as a royal or king. The first element is that of Jesus' entrance into the city by riding on a colt, a "not-yet-ridden" colt (11:2). It is dramatic and significant for two reasons. First, it was customary for Jewish pilgrims intending to enter the capital on foot. Moreover, as far as records do tell

---

64. Congar, *Temple*, 109. The Greek term for the vestibule, the holy place and the holy of holies is ναός.

65. Gray, *Temple*, 24–25.

us, Jesus has been approaching Jerusalem on foot as near as Jericho, where he has healed the blind Bartimaeus (10:46–52). But then, when he and his entourage of immediate disciples and crowd reach the Mount of Olives at Bethany and Bethphage (11:1), he stops, sends his two disciples to pick up a colt (probably at Bethphage, see above), and rides into the city, with the crowd's jubilant shouts and paving the road with their own cloaks and green leaves cut from the fields. This is not only dramatic; it is also extraordinary that a Jewish pilgrim would put on such an ostentatious entrance into Jerusalem on the eve of the Passover, unless of course, and now we are turning to the second point, that Jesus the pilgrim was not just that but also a royal. For, certainly, his dramatic and ostentatious entrance resembles entrances of royals and dignitaries of the ancient world. Culpepper has carefully studied and shown that "Jesus' entry into Jerusalem follows the well-established pattern of accounts of entrance processions."[66]

Paul Brooks Duff listed the characteristic elements of an ancient entrance processions:[67] (1) the conqueror is escorted into the city by citizenry or the army of the conqueror; (2) the procession is accompanied by hymns and/or acclamations; (3) the Roman triumph has shown us that various elements in the procession . . . symbolically depict the authority of the ruler; and (4) the entrance is followed by a ritual of appropriation, such as sacrifice, which takes place in the temple, whereby the ruler symbolically appropriates the city.

Here is Josephus's account (*B.J.* 11.332–36) of Alexander the Great's entrance into Jerusalem:

> Then all the Jews together greeted Alexander with one voice and surrounded him . . . [then] he gave his hand to the high priest and with the Jews running beside him, entered the city. Then he went up to the temple where he sacrificed to God under the direction of the high priest.[68]

Here is Plutarch's account (*Ant.* 24.3–4) of Anthony's entrance into Ephesus:

> When Antony made his entrance into Ephesus, women arrayed like Baccanals, and men and boys like satyrs and Pans, led the way before him, and the city was full of ivy and thyrsus-wands and harps and pipes and flutes, the people hailing him as Dionysius

---

66. Culpepper, *Mark*, 367.
67. Duff, "Divine Warrior."
68. Trans. Ralph Marcus, LCL.

Giver of Joy and Beneficent. For he was such undoubtedly, to some.[69]

Now having seen these two accounts and previously the common elements of royal entrances in the ancient world, let us go back and review Mark's account of Jesus' entry into Jerusalem. Which of the four characteristic elements listed are present? All four! First, Jesus, riding a colt, enters Jerusalem, escorted by his twelve apostles and the sympathetic and jubilant pilgrim crowd. Second, Jesus enters Jerusalem to the chant of the crowd, lifted from the Hallel Psalm 118:25-26a, "Hosanna! Blessed is he who comes in the name of the Lord!" (Mark 11:9). Third, the processional elements symbolizing Jesus' royalty include the colt itself, which Mark carefully describes as "not-yet-ridden," the people's cloaks and the leafy branches that they threw on the road for Jesus to pass. Fourth, Jesus enters the temple and, instead of offering a sacrifice, asserts his authority in God's house by driving out the sellers and buyers in the temple precincts and issues a rebuke and opposition to the temple leadership.

Next let us inquire into the Scriptural quotations and/or allusions in Mark's report of Jesus' riding on a colt into the Jewish capital and find out whether these further support the portrait of Jesus that we have so far seen, his royalty. The first of these allusions is connected with a basic detail in the Markan and parallel accounts: Jesus' riding on a colt into Jerusalem. It is worth noting that Mark did not quote Zech 9:9 ("Rejoice greatly, O daughter of Zion! ... See, your king comes to you ... gentle and riding on a donkey") where Matthew and John have quoted this OT text. Anderson has appealed to Wrede's "messianic secret" to explain Mark's awkward silence here.[70] Recent scholarship, however, is almost unanimous in saying that Mark is alluding to Zech 9. Hooker, who argues that we cannot be certain that Mark here is to be linked to Zech 9, nevertheless admits that Mark may have Zech 9 in mind when he wrote down this narrative.[71] Many other scholars[72] are enthusiastic in affirming the connection between Mark's colt and Zech 9. Hurtado argues strongly that Jesus' saddling a colt into Jerusa-

---

69. Trans. Bernadotte Perrin, LCL.
70. Anderson, *Gospel*, 261.
71. Hooker, *Commentary*, 257.
72. Van Iersel, *Mark*, 353; Alexander, *Mark*, 300; Donahue and Harrington, *Gospel*, 322; France, *Gospel*, 431, 434; Stein, *Mark*, 503-4; Chanikuzhy, *Jesus*, 103-4; Derrett, "Law," 257; Duff, "Divine Warrior," 55; Tatum, "Triumphal Entry"; Evans, *Mark 8:27—16:20*, 140.

lem is a "direct allusion to Zechariah 9:9."[73] Evans writes that Jesus' act "appears to be deliberately modeled after Zech 9:9.[74]" This OT text prophesies about the King of Zion coming to Jerusalem "riding on a donkey, on a colt, the foal of a donkey." It is therefore reasonable to conclude that in Mark's narrative Jesus who rides on a colt into Jerusalem is the prophesied King of Zion of Zech 9:9.

We find another allusion to the OT in Mark 11:8, where people spread their cloaks and the leaves they cut from the fields on the road where Jesus rides the colt. The OT passage that this alludes to is 2 Kgs 9:13, where it is said of King Jehu's coronation that people "hurried and took their cloaks and spread them under him on the bare steps. Then they blew the trumpet and shouted, 'Jehu is king!'" The spontaneous action of the crowd in Mark 11 parallels the great respect that the ancient Israelites accorded to their new king, Jehu. Lane finds such an action as "a spontaneous expression of homage to Jesus."[75] Though not all will share Lane's enthusiasm, nevertheless many scholars will accept that the crowd's action bespeaks their admiration and great respect for Jesus.[76] Taken singly, it will not establish Jesus' royalty. But taken together with the other royal connotations in Mark 11, then the crowd's action does enhance our picture of Jesus as the King of Zion.

Chanikuzhy, following J. D. M. Derrett, has seen a further evidence of Jesus' royalty in Mark 11:2 and following, where Jesus commands his two disciples to fetch a colt.[77] What Jesus does here, Chanikuzhy explains, "was in line with the royal right to 'impress'[78] (ἀνγγαρεία) beasts and even humans for the service of the ruler or the nation."[79] Jesus as king has the right to commandeer or requisition the colt. Chanikuzhy lists the following biblical references as cases of ἀνγγαρεία: 1 Sam 8:17; Matt 5:41; 27:32; and Mark 15:21. Apparently, however, this argument will work only if it can be clearly established that the ὁ κύριος of Mark 11:3 does indeed refer to Jesus.

---

73. Hurtado, *Mark*, 179.

74. Evans, *Mark 8:27—16:20*, 140.

75. Lane, *Lane*, 396.

76. Scholars like Hurtado, *Mark*, 179, Hooker, *Commentary*, 259, and Cranfield, *Gospel*, 350 simply interpret the crowd's action as a token of great respect.

77. Chanikuzhy, *Jesus*, 101.

78. Synonymous with "commandeer" and "requisition."

79. Chanikuzhy, , *Jesus*, 101.

But since ὁ κύριος here is ambiguous (it can refer to God,⁸⁰ Jesus,⁸¹ or the human owner of the colt⁸²), the ἀνγγαρεία concept of Mark 11:3 does not clearly prove Jesus' royalty.

The Theme of Messianism

Another important theme of Mark 11:1-10 is that of messianism. There are no doubt overlappings here with the features of royalty just discussed. The allusion to Zech 9:9 is as much an indication of royalty ("King of Zion") as it is of messianism, for the King of Zion is none other than the rightful heir to David's throne, the Son of David, the Messiah. But there are certainly other features of Mark 11:1-10 that do point to Jesus as the Messiah.

First, the reference to the Mount of Olives in Mark 11:1 is a messianic element based on the prophecy of Zech 14:4, "On that day ['the day of the LORD,' v. 1] his [the LORD's] feet will stand on the Mount of Olives . . ." France thinks it was not necessary for Mark to mention the Mount of Olives here because he already referred to Bethany and Bethphage, but that Mark mentioned it nonetheless because of its "messianic connotations."⁸³ Second, the expression ὁ ἐρχόμενος in Mark 11:9 has been viewed by certain scholars as messianic. Alexander states that it is "a beautiful description of the great deliverer so long expected."⁸⁴ Anderson acknowledges that this phrase no doubt "would have strong eschatological significance" for Mark and his readers.⁸⁵ Hooker argues more strongly in favor of the phrase's messianic significance by pointing to the parallel between the two greetings in verses 9 ("blessed is he who comes") and 10 ("blessed is the coming kingdom"). She writes, "The one who is welcomed [v. 9] also brings the kingdom [v. 10]."⁸⁶

Finally, ἡ βασιλεία τοῦ πατρὸς ἡμῶν Δαυίδ ("the kingdom of our father David," 11:10a) is also messianic. We may recall that just awhile ago, the blind Bartimaeus called Jesus "the Son of David," which Jesus apparently

---

80. Evans, *Mark 8:27—16:20*, 143; France, *Gospel of Mark*, 432.
81. Gundry, *Mark*, 624, 628; Hooker, *Commentary*, 258; Edwards, *Gospel*, 335; Stein, *Mark*, 504.
82. Taylor, *Gospel*, 454-55; Lane, *Gospel*, 391-92 n. 3; Cranfield, *Gospel*, 369.
83. France, *Gospel of Mark*, 430.
84. Alexander, *Mark*, 301.
85. Anderson, *Gospel*, 262.
86. Hooker, *Commentary*, 259-60 (emphasis added).

The Significance of the Marcan Temple Incident

accepted. Jesus did not rebuke Bartimaeus for calling him that—he tolerated him. This Bartimaeus, now healed, is presumably among the crowd shouting the coming of the kingdom of David. We cannot miss the clear associations here.[87] For Hooker, these "words serve to confirm the earlier proclamation of Jesus as the Son of David as he approached Jerusalem."[88]

SUMMARY

In Mark's account of the entry, Jesus comes and presents himself to Jerusalem—the nation's capital and the seat of Jewish leadership—as the King of Zion (Zech 9:9), the rightful heir to David's throne, even as he himself is the Son of David as affirmed by Bartimaeus in 10:47–48, the Messiah. Jesus enters the holy city saddling on a donkey, to the jubilant chants and welcome by the enthusiastic pilgrim crowd who serve as the harmless army of this Davidic king. The crowd shouts, "Hosanna! Blessed is he who comes in the name of the Lord. Blessed is the coming kingdom of our father David. Hosanna in the highest!" But the city snubs the King. With this anticlimactic ending, Mark 11:1–11 portrays the fateful tension between Jesus and the Jewish leaders which unravels in the remainder of Mark's narrative.

The Cursing of the Fig Tree (vv. 12–14, 20–26)

Another significant context for Jesus' temple incident in Mark's (as well as Matthew's) narrative is the cursing of the fig tree. Mark's presentation of this incident differs from Matthew's on two counts. First, Jesus curses the fig before his dramatic action in the temple, and the apostles report on the following day that the cursed fig tree withers, whereas in Matthew these events happened on the same day as the temple incident. Second, whereas Matthew presents the cursing of the fig tree as one unified event (21:18–22), Mark splits it into two parts (11:12–14; 11:20–26) and inserts Jesus' temple act (11:15–19) in the middle. This sandwich structure[89] implies that the cursing of the fig tree explains the meaning of Jesus' action in the temple

---

87. Van Iersel, *Mark*, 354.

88. Hooker, *Commentary*, 260. Hurtado seems to be noncommittal in his interpretation of the phrase: "The cry about the coming kingdom of our father David is no doubt a reference to the ancient Jewish prayer that God would send the Messiah, the Son of David, who would restore the kingship to Israel as in David's time" (*Mark*, 180).

89. A similar structure is found in Mark 5:21–43.

The Significance of the Temple Incident in the Narratives of the Four Gospels

and vice versa. Hooker has pointed out that this (smaller) sandwich structure (11:12–21) is in fact within a larger, more complex sandwich structure of Mark 11:1–11 (Jesus' entry into Jerusalem) and 11:27–33 (Jesus' authority questioned) dealing with Jesus' identity and authority.[90] Right away we get a handle of what Mark 11 is all about—Jesus is the Messiah whom Israel rejects and the conflict that issues from such a confrontation.[91]

Certain scholars have found difficulty accepting the historicity of this account. Manson considers this incident "a tale of miraculous power wasted in the service of ill-temper . . . as it stands it is simply incredible."[92] Schwartz thinks that this account "had its origin in a local legend concerning a withered fig tree in the vicinity of Bethany . . ."[93] The main difficulties in the texts are twofold. First, Jesus' cursing a fig tree appears out of sync with his character. Why would he curse the tree for not having fruit? France observes that Jesus' action here appears to be "spiteful," "vindictive," and a "misuse" of his miraculous power.[94] Second, the difficulty is compounded by Mark's comment in verse 13 that it was not the season for figs to bear fruit. Why would Jesus curse the tree for not having fruit if it was not the tree's season for fruit-bearing?

These difficulties can be explained and Jesus' action can start to make sense when (1) we understand and appreciate what the fig tree symbolically stands for in the Hebrew Scriptures and (2) understand Mark's parenthetical comment in verse 13, ὁ γὰρ καιρὸς οὐκ ἦν σύκων ("for it was not the season for figs"). Fig trees and their fruit are employed by the OT prophets to symbolize Israel and her deeds of obedience (Isa 28:3–4; Jer 8:13; Hosea 9:10, 16; Joel 1:7, 12; Mic 7:1).[95] Knowledge of this symbolism was pervasive in Judaism so that the Jews of Jesus' time, such as Mark and his

---

90. Hooker, *Commentary*, 261.

91. Also helpful four our grasping the big picture is France's (*Gospel of Mark*, 436) arrangement of 11:11–27.

    A First visit to the *temple* (11:11)
        B Cursing of the *fig tree* (11:12–14)
    A Jesus takes action in the *temple* (11:15–19)
        B The *fig tree* is found to be dead (11:20–25)
    A Jesus returns to the *temple* (11:27)

92. Manson, "Cleansing," 279.

93. Cited in Lane, *Gospel*, 399.

94. France, *Gospel of Mark*, 439.

95. See Telford (*Temple*, 132–63) for a helpful survey of the symbolic use of the fig tree in the OT, and 179–96 for a study of fig trees' symbolic use in post-biblical Judaism.

readers, would have easily understood the intended point once Jesus shows frustration at the sight of a fruitless fig tree.⁹⁶ Mark's comment in verse 13, ὁ γὰρ καιρὸς οὐκ ἦν σύκων, further leads toward the symbolic interpretation of this incident. One effect of that comment, as has been noted, is to compound the seeming inconsistency in this passage: why would Jesus, who himself knew the seasons for the fig trees' fruit-bearing, blame the tree for not bearing fruit outside of its appointed season? Mark's comment thus points us toward a symbolic take of this incident. Hooker calls Mark's comment "a deliberate hint to us to take the story symbolically."⁹⁷ Lane writes, "The unexpected and incongruous character of Jesus' action in looking for figs at a season when no fruit could be found would stimulate curiosity and point beyond the incident to its deeper significance."⁹⁸ In effect, Mark was saying, "Even though Jesus knew that it was not the fig tree's season to bear fruit, he still went to inspect the tree for fruit, for he was trying to illustrate by it the condition of Israel. From afar, the tree, covered with leaves, had the appearance of fruitfulness. But on close inspection, it was fruitless. This tree symbolizes Israel, who had the appearance of good health, but on close inspection, it was empty."

The subsequent events must also be interpreted in the same way. Jesus' cursing of the fig tree symbolizes God's verdict on Israel: the nation would be destroyed, Jerusalem would fall, and the temple would vanish. The withering of the fig tree from its roots symbolizes the utter destruction of the temple and its institution.

ANALYSIS OF THE MARCAN TEMPLE INCIDENT PERICOPE⁹⁹

Greek Text, Translation, and Structure

Greek text:

> 15 Καὶ ἔρχονται εἰς Ἱεροσόλυμα. καὶ εἰσελθὼν εἰς τὸ ἱερὸν ἤρξατο ἐκβάλλειν τοὺς πωλοῦντας καὶ τοὺς ἀγοράζοντας ἐν τῷ ἱερῷ, καὶ

---

96. So Hooker, *Commentary*, 262; France, *Gospel of Mark*, 439.
97. Hooker, *Commentary*, 262.
98. Lane, *Gospel*, 400.
99. Refer to Appendix 2 for a color-coded comparison of the Synoptic Gospels' accounts of Jesus' temple act. Also refer to Appendix 3 for a comparison of Mark's and John's accounts of the incident.

τὰς τραπέζας τῶν κολλυβιστῶν καὶ τὰς καθέδρας τῶν πωλούντων τὰς περιστερὰς κατέστρεψεν, 16 καὶ οὐκ ἤφιεν ἵνα τις διενέγκῃ σκεῦος διὰ τοῦ ἱεροῦ. 17 καὶ ἐδίδασκεν καὶ ἔλεγεν αὐτοῖς, Οὐ γέγραπται ὅτι Ὁ οἶκός μου οἶκος προσευχῆς κληθήσεται πᾶσιν τοῖς ἔθνεσιν; ὑμεῖς δὲ πεποιήκατε αὐτὸν σπήλαιον λῃστῶν. 18 καὶ ἤκουσαν οἱ ἀρχιερεῖς καὶ οἱ γραμματεῖς, καὶ ἐζήτουν πῶς αὐτὸν ἀπολέσωσιν· ἐφοβοῦντο γὰρ αὐτόν, πᾶς γὰρ ὁ ὄχλος ἐξεπλήσσετο ἐπὶ τῇ διδαχῇ αὐτοῦ. 19 Καὶ ὅταν ὀψὲ ἐγένετο, ἐξεπορεύοντο[100] ἔξω τῆς πόλεως.

Translation:

15 And they came to Jerusalem. And having entered the temple he began to drive out those who were selling and buying in the temple, and he overthrew the tables of the moneychangers and the seats of those who sold doves. 16 And he would not permit any man to carry a vessel through the temple. 17 And he taught and said to them, "Is it not written, 'My house shall be called a house of prayer for all the nations'? But you have made it a den of robbers." 18 And the chief priests and the scribes heard it, and they sought how they might destroy him, for the whole crowd was amazed at his teaching. 19 And when evening came, they went out of the city.

Structure and Outline

We can outline the thought flow of Mark 11:15–18 as follows.[101]

1. Jesus reenters Jerusalem and the temple (v. 15a; cf. v. 11).

2. Jesus protests in the temple (vv. 15b–16).

3. Jesus teaches in the temple (v. 17).

4. The chief priests and scribes plot against Jesus (v. 18).

---

100. Other manuscripts have ἐξεπορεύετο ("he went out"). This is difficult to resolve on the basis of attestation since both have strong support. But considering verse 15a, καὶ ἔρχονται εἰς Ἱεροσόλυμα, we may understand Mark to mean that Jesus also went out of the city in the company of his disciples.

101. See Gundry, *Mark*, 639.

Textual Analysis

Jesus Reenters Jerusalem and the Temple (v. 15a)

It is better to translate verse 15a as "Jesus and his disciples returned to Jerusalem" because just the day before this, Jesus had ostentatiously—riding on a donkey to the jubilant shouts of his accompanying pilgrim crowd—entered the city and inspected the temple. Things are still very fresh and now he returns to the city. He returns because he has an unfinished business with the city, specifically with the temple, as indicated by Mark's abrupt and seemingly anticlimactic 11:11. We recall that when Jesus entered the city, intentionally presenting himself as the royal Messiah, Jerusalem was ominously quiet, which was totally opposite to the crowd's acclamation of Jesus outside the city walls. As far as Mark is concerned, Jerusalem did not care about Jesus; the city did not even care to ask the question, "Who is this?" (Matt 21:10). This rejection of the Messiah left a deep mark on Jesus' heart, and so on the following day Jesus' performed a prophetic sign-act in the sight of his disciples: he cursed the seemingly fruitful yet fruitless fig tree. Without a doubt the disciples understood that fruitless fig tree as symbolizing Israel. Jesus' unfinished business with Israel is exactly that—Jesus as Israel's Messiah-King will continue to confront the Jewish nation with who he is, and the stubborn unbelief of the Jews will ensure that this confrontation will be dramatic and deadly. Jesus' action in the temple is to be seen in this light.

Jesus Protests in the Temple (vv. 15b–16)

Jesus wastes no time. After entering the city, he goes directly into the temple and begins to perform dramatic acts there. The term for temple used here, ἱερὸν, suggests that these dramatic actions were performed "in the outer courts accessible to pagans, with the porticos" such as "the Royal Portico on the southern boundary, with its three hundred and sixty columns and its three aisles; Solomon's Porch stretching along the eastern boundary and dominating the Valley of the Cedron."[102] Jesus was quite familiar with these places as he probably had often taught here. As we have noted in our comments on Matthew's narrative of the temple incident, the temple became abuzz with activities and people on Jewish national feasts such as this one,

---

102. Congar, *Temple*, 109.

the Passover. These outer courts became market places, with all business transactions connected with the temple cult. Verse 15 mentions "those who were buying and selling in the temple," "the money-changers," and "those who sold doves." Of the sellers, Gundry writes, "The sellers sell sacrificial animals guaranteed to be clean to pilgrims who live too far away to bring their own and to locals who do not want to risk having their own animals declared unclean by priestly inspectors."[103] Money-changing services were also needed in the temple because only the Tyrian currency was acceptable for paying the annual half-shekel temple tax that was required of each Jewish male twenty-one years of age or older, and also those who needed to buy sacrificial animals could only do so using this prescribed currency. According to Stein, "money-changing tables were set up in the provinces surrounding Jerusalem on the fifteenth day of Adar, the month preceding Passover. On the twenty-fifth of that month, they were set up in the Court of the Gentiles (*m. Suk.* 1.1, 3) so that the tax could be paid by the first of Nisan (the next month), although late payment was common (*m. Suk.* 1.6)."[104] Stein adds that money-exchange service involved a charge of about 4–8 percent. Selling doves in the temple was for those who could not afford animals.

Another dramatic act of Jesus is recorded in verse 16: "And he would not permit any man to carry a vessel (σκεῦος) through the temple." This is unique to Mark. The word σκεῦος has several meanings (i.e. "utensil," "instrument," "household stuff," "furniture," "goods," and so on), but in Mark 11:16 (as in also in Luke 8:16 and Rom 9:21) it means "a vessel, utensil for containing anything."[105] That definition is supported by BDAG which translates σκεῦος as a "thing, object used for any purpose at all."[106] Jesus' prohibition of this kind of traffic in the temple conforms to a similar prohibition in the Mishnah: A man "may not enter into the Temple with his staff or his sandal or his wallet, or with the dust upon his feet, nor may he make of it a short by-path; still less may he spit there" (*Ber.* 9.5).

---

103. Gundry, *Mark*, 642.
104. Stein, *Mark*, 515.
105. Perschbacher, *Lexicon*, 371.
106. J. M. Ford ("Money Bags") argues that the term refers to "money-bags" in the temple. But this is lexically unconvincing (see France, *Gospel of Mark*, 445 n. 58).

Jesus Teaches in the Temple (v. 17)

Jesus here quotes from two OT passages and Mark understood this (as indicated by his use of ἐδίδασκεν) as Jesus' "teaching" activity. For Anderson, the phrase ἐδίδασκεν καὶ ἔλεγεν is a "Markan formula which shows the real importance for him of the Temple cleansing episode. Jesus' cleansing of the Temple is thus brought by Mark under the cover of his teaching activity."[107] Hooker correctly pointed out that the phrase indicates Mark's understanding that what Jesus was about to say was the basis of his protest.[108] The first quotation comes from Isa 56:7, an exact equivalent of the LXX: Ὁ οἶκός μου οἶκος προσευχῆς κληθήσεται πᾶσιν τοῖς ἔθνεσιν. Both Matthew and Luke omit πᾶσιν τοῖς ἔθνεσιν—and this observation is crucial for our exegesis of the Markan text. The second part of Mark 11:17, ὑμεῖς δὲ πεποιήκατε αὐτὸν σπήλαιον λῃστῶν ("but you have made it a den of robbers"), alludes to Jer 7:11.

The Chief Priests and Scribes Plot against Jesus (v. 18)

If Jesus' action in the temple had a concrete result, it was that it pushed the Jewish leaders' opposition against him to a deadly level. The chief priests (οἱ ἀρχιερεῖς) and the scribes (οἱ γραμματεῖς) were two of the three classes (the third was οἱ πρεσβύτεροι) that composed the Sanhedrin, the Jewish supreme council, in Mark's narrative. Οἱ ἀρχιερεῖς was a group which included the high priest, the "other priest" who was to assume the role of the high priest in case of emergency, the retired high priests, the captain of the temple, and the temple treasurer.[109] The scribes (οἱ γραμματεῖς), otherwise known in the Gospels as *nomikoi* ("lawyers") or *nomodidaskaloi* ("teachers of the law"),[110] "were recognized as authoritative teachers of Jewish law and custom (1:22; 9:11)."[111] Saldarini believes that their role "seems to be as associates of the priests, both in judicial proceeding and enforcement of

---

107. Anderson, *Gospel*, 266. Stein (*Mark*, 517) suggests that the imperfect ἐδίδασκεν καὶ ἔλεγεν indicates that Jesus was teaching while carrying out his protest, but that is not certain.

108. Hooker, *Commentary*, 268.

109. Evans, *Mark*, 179–80; also Stein, *Mark*, 518.

110. Unger, *Dictionary*, 1543.

111. Saldarini, "Scribes," 1015.

Jewish custom and law, and ongoing business in the Sanhedrin."[112] The chief priests, the scribes, and the elders figure prominently in Mark's narrative of Jesus' last week in Jerusalem, and it is as one body, the Sanhedrin, that they pushed to end Jesus' life. What Mark 11:18 makes clear is that "Jesus' action in the temple court before Passover moved him into the cross-hairs of Jerusalem's priests, and sealed his fate."[113]

Distinguishing Features of Mark 11:15–19

Among the Synoptic Gospels, Mark has the longest account of Jesus' temple act, followed by Matthew, and then Luke. The specific distinctives of Mark's account are as follows. First, Mark 11:16, καὶ οὐκ ἤφιεν ἵνα τις διενέγκῃ σκεῦος διὰ τοῦ ἱεροῦ ("And he would not permit any one to carry a vessel through the temple"), has no parallel in either Matthew or Luke, and not even in John. Second, Mark specifically notes that Jesus taught (ἐδίδασκεν) in the temple (not even John has this note). Third, Mark's Jesus quotes Isa 56:11 more fully, including πᾶσιν τοῖς ἔθνεσιν ("for all the nations"), which is omitted in both Matthew and Luke.

Mark 11:16 is a crucial text for its presence in Mark and for its absence in the other Gospels. We should notice first of all Jesus' display of authority here: "He would not permit anyone to carry a vessel through the temple." This is consistent with the authority he displayed earlier in verse 15. He is here acting as the temple chief who has authority to effect changes to the activities in the temple and to the way the temple is used.[114] In fact, as we have already seen in Mark 11:1–11, it is as the Messiah-King that Jesus presented himself to Jerusalem and the temple. It is with such authority that he here issues the prohibition in Mark 11:16, needing no clearance from the Jewish leaders. Yes, Jesus took over the authority of ruling the temple, even if very briefly. Yes, by his actions he showed no regard or respect for the temple leadership. Later, these leaders would confront Jesus exactly on this question of authority: "By what authority are you doing these things? And who gave you the authority to do this?" (Mark 11:28).

---

112. Saldarini, "Scribes," 1015.

113. Fredriksen, "Chronologies," 247. So also Brandon, *Jesus*, 334–36; Juel, *Messiah*, 127–42; Sanders, *Jesus*, 61–90; Cranfield, *Gospel*, 378. Wright (*Jesus*, 414) writes: "What [Jesus] did in the Temple was closely integrated with, perhaps even climactic to, the rest of his work."

114. See Perkins, "Gospel," 663.

Another important point from Mark 11:16 lies with the word σκεῦος, whose plain meaning is "vessel" or "container." Scholars have debated the meaning of this word because of its importance: What did Jesus prohibit from being carried "through" the temple? The NIV translates it as "merchandise," a meaning related to the business transactions going on the temple courts—"selling and buying" and money-changing (v. 14). Other versions such as the KJV prefer the plain meaning "vessel." The meaning we assign to this word affects our understanding of the other aspects of the temple act, and that explains scholars' preoccupation with this word. One group of scholars, such as Cranfield[115] and Hooker,[116] defines σκεῦος as "any goods." The point of Jesus' prohibition, they contend, is that Jesus did not want to continue to see people (particularly Jerusalem residents) disrespecting the temple by using it as a shortcut in carrying or transporting their goods.[117] Another group of scholars defines σκεῦος as "cultic vessel."[118] The common explanation for this is given by Telford: "Jesus' action then, according to Mark, was aimed directly against the sacrificial cultus, there being no more effective means of stopping the flow of sacrifices than seizing the vessels in which gifts and offerings were received by the priests (on behalf of worshipers) *through* the various Temple porticos to the altar."[119]

This second definition is what this paper adopts. The main argument is that to define σκεῦος as "cultic vessel" coheres well with the import of the cursing of the fig tree, which symbolizes the eschatological destruction of the temple. Not only the overturning of the money-changers' tables and the seats of the dove-sellers that symbolizes the temple's destruction but also Jesus' hijacking of the traffic of temple vessels; both of these actions were prophetically symbolic actions that spoke the imminent and utter destruction of the temple, and they both cohere with the fig tree cursing.

The second distinctive feature of the Marcan temple incident is the reference to Jesus' teaching activity in 11:17, ἐδίδασκεν καὶ ἔλεγεν αὐτοῖς, whereas all the other Gospels simply say ἔλεγεν αὐτοῖς. Two other

---

115. Cranfield, *Gospel*, 358.

116. Hooker, *Commentary*, 268.

117. Cranfield (*Gospel*, 358) quotes from the *m. Ber.* 9:5, a man "may not enter into the Temple Mount with his staff or his sandal or his wallet, or with the dust upon his feet, nor may he make of it a short by-path; still less may he spit there."

118. Kelber, *Kingdom*, 145–47; Gray, *Temple*, 28–30; and Gundry, *Mark*, 642–43.

119. Telford, *Temple*, 93 n. 102. Bauckham ("Demonstration," 78) also explains: "The vessels were not being carried from one outer gate of the temple to another, but through the temple from the outer court to the store-chambers in the court of women."

occasions where Mark referenced Jesus' teaching is in 1:21–28, where Jesus went into the local synagogue in Capernaum and taught. Mark reports that "the people were amazed at his teaching, because he taught them as one who had authority, not as the teachers of the law" (v. 22, repeated in v. 27, "the people were all so amazed"), and in 6:1–3, where Jesus taught in his hometown synagogue and "many who heard him were amazed" (v. 2). Here in the temple incident account, the reason why Mark makes reference to Jesus' teaching activity (11:17) is that he wants to alert us to one reason why the chief priests and the teachers of the law want to kill Jesus—"for they feared him, because the whole crowd was amazed at his teaching" (v. 18b).

It was E. P. Sanders, with the publication of *Jesus and Judaism* in 1985, who shifted the focus of discussion from Jesus' statements (Mark 11:17) to Jesus' deed (Mark 11:15f.). Sanders did not focus on 11:17 because it was his conviction that this text did not come out from Jesus' lips but a later addition by the Christian community,[120] and only 11:15–16 reflects original actions by Jesus. As a result of this, Sanders's interpretation of Jesus' temple act—that Jesus' overturning the tables symbolically proclaimed the temple's impending destruction—is exclusively based on 11:15–16, without consideration of 11:17–18. But Sanders has missed a significant point here because, even as he himself argues that Jesus' action in the temple courts moved the Jewish leaders to move decisively to kill Jesus, Mark in 11:18 does indeed affirm that they plotted to kill Jesus because the crowds were spellbound at his teaching, and this teaching must include both Jesus' actions in 11:15–16 and his words in 11:17, just as in 1:21–28 Jesus' teaching also included both action (exorcising demons) and verbal instructions.

The third distinctive feature of Mark's account of the temple incident is the more complete quotation of Isa 56:7 to include the words πᾶσιν τοῖς ἔθνεσιν ("for all the nations"). This quotation seems to indicate Mark's particular concern for Gentiles.[121] In Jesus' discourse concerning the signs of the end of the age, Mark in 13:10 records Jesus as saying that "the gospel must be preached to all the nations." Mark also records for us that it was the centurion, a Gentile, who supervised Jesus' crucifixion, who was the first to dramatically come to faith in Jesus right after his death on the cross (15:39). As to the original context of Isa 56:7, we find in 56:1–2 a call to justice, in

---

120. Sanders, *Jesus*, 66. One of Sanders's sources is Roloff who also concluded, based on Mark's editorial comment "and he taught them and said," that Mark 11:17 is a later addition by the early church.

121. Juel, *Messiah*, 131–32; France, *Gospel Mark*, 445–46.

56:3–8 a call to covenant, and in 56:9–12 God's condemnation against the wicked. Isaiah 56:7 says,

> These I will bring to my holy mountain and make them joyful in my house of prayer; their burnt offerings and their sacrifices will be accepted on my altar; for my house shall called a house of prayer for all peoples.

What we have here is "a series of promises that in the coming age foreigners and other outsiders will enjoy full rights in the worship of God in Jerusalem."[122] Isaiah 56:7 draws "all peoples" into a covenant relationship with Yahweh.[123] This of course has two inevitable implications. First, the temple current to Jesus' time has failed to become "a house of prayer for all peoples"; instead, it has become "a den of robbers." Second, how the temple has become a den of robbers[124] is connected to Jesus' action in Mark 11:15, where right there in the temple precincts, the only areas in the temple compound where Gentiles had access, worship was drowned by the busy and noisy mercantile activities.

SUMMARY AND CONCLUSION

We have seen that Mark 11 is unified by the theme of authority and conflict (controversy)—Jesus' authority, the Jewish leaders' authority, and the conflict arising from the clash of these two authorities. This theme is carried on to the remaining chapters of the book, leading up to Jesus' suffering and death. Mark 11, then, signals the beginning of the passion week.

We have also learned that Mark 11 employs two "sandwich" structures. The bigger sandwich structure has Jesus' entry into Jerusalem (11:1–11) and the Jewish leaders' questioning Jesus' authority (11:27–33) as the two halves of the sandwich and 11:12–26 as the meat inside. The smaller "sandwich" structure involves Mark 11:12–26. The cursing of the fig tree (11:12–14) and the withering of that tree (11:20–25) serve to contain in the middle Jesus' action in the temple (11:15–19). This way of structuring Mark 11 yields in Jesus' temple act as the core of the whole chapter. The implication of this sandwich structure is quite significant. In the case of the smaller "sandwich" structure, Jesus' temple act (11:15–19) is interpreted by

---

122. France, *Gospel of Mark*, 445.
123. Qualls, "Mark," 398.
124. My view of the term robber has been set out in chapter 2.

the cursing of the fig tree (11:12–14) and its withering (11:20–25), and vice versa. This mutual interpretive interaction of course also applies to other sandwich structures in Mark.

What is the function of Jesus' temple act in Mark's narrative? We note some key points. First, what scholars (named above) have concluded is true that Jesus' action in the temple was the main event that sealed his fate with the Jewish authorities. Mark 11:18 tells us that after the "chief priests" and the "scribes" heard about Jesus' action in the temple, they began to look for a way to kill him (cf. 12:12; 14:1, 43; and so on).

Second, Mark's presentation of Jesus' temple act is so dramatic and action-filled, and if we add this to Mark's equally dramatic report of Jesus' entry into the city on the previous day, we get a portrait of Jesus as the Messiah-King who is deeply aware and conscious of his own identity and mission and who is eager to press his claims on Jerusalem and the temple. Indeed, Mark like no other evangelists portrays the dramatic encounter between the Messiah-King Jesus and the unbelieving Jewish authorities.

Third, in keeping with the meaning of the cursing and withering of the fig tree (11:12–14, 20–25), Jesus' temple act is correctly understood as a prophetic gesture symbolizing God's authoritative judgment on Jerusalem and the temple. Jesus' coming to the temple is to be understood as a "divine inspection."[125] Just as Jesus found no fruit on the tree despite its appearances to the contrary (full of leaves), he also did not find any good fruit in Israel despite her appearances of external health and holiness. Just as Jesus cursed the tree and it withered from the roots, so too did Jesus curse Jerusalem and the temple and declare its utter destruction.

Finally, Mark's inclusion of πᾶσιν τοῖς ἔθνεσιν not only indicates Mark's focus on Gentiles but also shows the guilt of the temple authorities, for, instead of making the temple "a house of prayer for all the nations," they made the temple precincts "a den of robbers." They thus deserved Jesus' righteous and omnipotent judgment. Πᾶσιν τοῖς ἔθνεσιν also serves here as a prophecy pointing to the soon fulfillment of God's desire that all nations should be able to worship him (Isa 56:7). That of course has been realized as a result of Jesus' death and resurrection, through which Jews and Gentiles alike are joined together to constitute the church of which Jesus is the head.

How did the temple incident make sense to readers who lived under intense Neronian persecution in the mid-60s? On the surface of it, this pericope seems to be irrelevant to such readers. But then we recall that in

---

125. Walker, *Jesus*, 4.

the Marcan narrative, it is Jesus' temple act that serves as the precipitating cause for the Jewish leaders to plot against Jesus (cf. 11:18). Now we begin to see the profound relevance of this pericope to the Markan community. After his protest at the temple, Jesus was a marked man. In a matter of a few days, the Jewish opposition to Jesus would intensify and culminate in him being hung on the cross. There he died. Mark closely attached the temple incident to Jesus' suffering and death. This emphasis on suffering and cross-bearing would have been picked up by the Markan community. If their Lord and Savior walked the pathway of suffering, then they themselves need not despair the persecution emanating from their hostile surroundings. These readers would have known and understood that the Jewish opposition to Jesus paralleled the Roman persecution and opposition. They would have pictured Jesus as partaking in their suffering and they in his suffering. Suffering, however, was not the end, for Jesus rose again and was vindicated and glorified. The Markan community would have found so much hope, strength, and encouragement from the risen Lord.

4

The Significance of the Lucan Temple Incident

CONTEXTUAL CONSIDERATION[1]

OUR PURPOSE IN THIS chapter is to grasp the significance of the Lucan temple incident (19:45–46) by the use of a compositional analysis. The same procedures as in chapters 2 and 3 will be followed here. The first step will be to grasp the "big picture" of Luke. The same questions as in above will be investigated. In step two, we will consider the immediate context of Luke's account of the temple incident (19:45–46), namely Jesus' entry into Jerusalem (19:28–40), Jesus' lament over Jerusalem (19:41–44), and Jesus' daily teaching at the temple (19:47–48). We will then study the temple incident itself (19:45–46), understanding its language, determining its structure, and identifying its key themes and emphases. Then in the final step, we will take a step back and find out how these themes and emphases cohere with the overall message and emphases of Luke's Gospel. We will then be able to express the meaning or significance of the temple incident in the narrative of Luke.

---

1. Refer to Appendix 1 for a comparison of the contextual locations of the temple incident in the Gospels.

Luke's overall Message and Emphases

The case for Lucan authorship of the third Gospel is strong. We can build up this case in the following steps. In terms of internal evidence, we infer from the Gospel's prologue (1:1–4) that its author was not a witness to Jesus' earthly life and ministry. So automatically the apostles are counted out of the options. Another internal evidence is the numerous "we" passages in Acts such as 16:10–17; 20:5–15; 21:1–18; 27:1—28:16. That implies that the author of Luke-Acts was an associate of Paul. The apostle Paul had many associates, such as Mark, Aristarchus, Demas, Luke, Timothy, Titus, Silas, Epaphras, and Barnabas. The list is long, so who is it? Here the testimonies of the early church come in handy.

The oldest surviving copy of the third Gospel, Papyrus Bodmer XIV (P^{75}, dating from 175–225 CE),[2] named Luke as the author of this Gospel.[3] When we survey other literature of the early church, we are astonished at the vast unanimity of the third Gospel's attribution to Lucan authorship. Justin Martyr (ca. 160, *Dial.* 103.19) speaks of Luke writing a "memoir of Jesus" and notes that the author is a follower of Paul. The Muratorian Canon (ca. 170–180) testifies, "After the ascension of Christ, Luke, whom Paul had taken with him as an expert in the way, wrote under his own name and according to his own understanding. He had not, of course, seen the Lord in the flesh, and therefore he begins to tell the story from the birth of John on, insofar as it was accessible to him."[4] Irenaeus (ca. 175–195, *Haer.* 3.1.1; 3.14.1) also attributes the second Gospel to Luke, follower of Paul, and notes how the "we" sections of Acts suggest this connection. The so-called *Anti-Marcionite Prologue* to Luke (ca. 175) describes Luke as a native of Antioch in Syria (Acts 11:19–30; 13:1–3; 15:30–35). It says that Luke lived to be 84, was a doctor, was unmarried, wrote in Achaia, and died in Boeotia. Eusebius (early fourth century, *Hist. eccl.* 3.4.2) mentions Luke as a companion of Paul, a native of Antioch, and author of the third Gospel and Acts. Considering all these testimonies, we have a well-founded confidence that Luke indeed penned the twin volume of Luke-Acts.

When did Luke write his Gospel? The predominant view of critical scholars is a post-70 CE date.[5] J. A. T. Robinson is quite notable and ex-

---

2. Fitzmyer, "Aramaic Evidence," 114–15.
3. See Tannehill, *Luke*, 20.
4. Quoted in Knight, *Gospel*, 9–10.
5. For example, Brown (*Introduction*, 226) dates Luke at 85 CE. See also Brown,

ceptional as a liberal scholar, for he dated almost all NT books prior to 70 CE.[6] His reason for doing so is that the NT makes no reference to the destruction of Jerusalem in 70 CE. If any NT book, for example Luke, was written after 70 CE, it is difficult to reckon why that book would not refer to this profoundly important and significant event. Robinson, therefore, was willing to grant that passages such as Luke 21 were prophetic (foretelling), which is a very conservative reading.

Of course, besides the absence of any reference to the destruction of Jerusalem in 70 CE, there are other arguments in favor of a pre-70 date for Luke's composition. Carson and Moo lists them as follows.[7] First, Acts makes no reference to the Neronian persecution of the mid-60s and the deaths of Peter and Paul. Second, the ending of Acts tells of Paul's imprisonment but not of his death (martyrdom). Third, if the evangelist Luke makes reference to the fulfillment of Agabus's prophecy of a world-wide famine (Acts 11:28), and if he wrote after the fall of Jerusalem, why did he not refer to this most crucial event? Fourth, "the most probable reading of the Pastoral Epistles is that Paul was released from his Roman custody described at the end of Acts and returned to the Eastern Mediterranean for further ministry." Fifth, the Pauline epistles were treasured in the early church, but why does Acts makes no reference to them? Finally, "it is questioned whether a Christian writer would give as friendly a picture of Rome as we find in Luke-Acts after the Neronian persecution." The weight of the combined evidence allows us to date Luke's composition in the early 60s or even earlier than that as in the 50s.[8]

For whom did Luke write his Gospel and why? Luke is plain and explicit about this. The Gospel's prologue (1:1–4)[9] identifies both the recipient and purpose.

> 1 Since many have undertaken to set down an orderly account of the events that have been fulfilled among us, 2 just as they were

---

Apostasy, 273–74; Fitzmyer, *Gospel*, 1:53–57.

6. Robinson, *Redating*.

7. Carson and Moo, *Introduction*, 207–8.

8. Morris, *Gospel*, 22–26; Marshall, *Gospel*, 33–35; Bock, *Luke*, 1:16–18; Carson and Moo, *Introduction*, 207–8.

9. Various scholars have pointed out that Luke's prologue, unparalleled by the other Gospels, has parallels in the "classical prefaces of Greek historians (Herodotus, Thucydides) and of the Hellenistic medical and scientific treatises or manuals" (Brown, *Introduction*, 227; see also Cadbury, *Commentary*, 2:489–510; Robbins, "Preface"; Dillon, "Luke's Project"; Callan, "Preface"; Alexander "Preface"; Alexander, *Preface*.

handed down to us by those who from the beginning were eyewitnesses and servants of the word, 3 I too decided, after investigating everything carefully from the very first, to write an orderly account for you, most excellent Theophilus, 4 so that you may know the truth concerning the things about which you have been instructed.[10]

The way Luke addresses Theophilus here—"most excellent"—suggests that Theophilus was a definite individual,[11] a man of rank, and a new Christian.[12] But of course it is likely that Luke had also intended his Gospel to be read and be a blessing to wider audiences. There are indications in the Gospel of the author's anticipation of Gentile readership beyond Theophilus who himself was also a Gentile. Notable are the following: the author's concern to situate key Gospel events in the context of secular history (e.g., 2:1; 3:1–2); his emphasis on the universal implications of the gospel (e.g., his genealogy of Christ goes back to Adam vis-à-vis Matthew's that goes back to Abraham); his omission of materials that focus on the Jewish law (e.g., the antitheses of Matt 5; the controversy about "uncleanness" [Mark 7:1– 23]); his tendency to substitute Greek equivalents to Jewish titles (e.g., "Lord" or "Teacher" for "Rabbi"); and his focus on Gentile coverts in the book of Acts.[13]

The question of why Luke wrote his Gospel[14] brings us back to the prologue, where he says that he writes "an orderly account" of "the things that had been fulfilled among us"—referring to Jesus' life and ministry—in order that the most excellent Theophilus "may know the certainty of the things he has been taught" (1:1–4). Luke did not write to evangelize Theophilus. A historian and a well-educated man, Luke wrote an account of Jesus for Theophilus's spiritual and intellectual benefit. Theophilus, perhaps a God-fearer prior to becoming a Christian,[15] might have faced some problem affecting his faith in Jesus. After his conversion, as he started to associate himself with the Christian movement, particularly a local congregation,

---

10. Consider also Acts 1:1: "In the first book, Theophilus, I wrote about all that Jesus did and taught from the beginning."

11. Alexander, *Preface*, 188; Stein, *Luke*, 26.

12. Carson and Moo (*Introduction*, 210) suggest that Theophilus "may have been Luke's patron, the person who incurred the costs of Luke's writing."

13. See Carson and Moo, *Introduction*, 211; Fitzmyer, *Gospel*, 1:58–59.

14. See Bock, *Luke*, 1:14; and Maddox, *Purpose*, 20–22 for a summary of the plethora of suggestions for Luke's purpose.

15. Theophilus literally means "beloved of God."

doubts started to surface whether he really belonged to this racially mixed and heavily persecuted community. Bock explains,

> The detail in Luke-Acts about faithfulness, Jew-Gentile relations, and clinging to the hope of Jesus' return suggests a Gentile who is experiencing doubt about his association with the new community. The problems over table fellowship, Gentile inclusion, and examples of how rejection was faced in the early church suggests this setting... In the Gospel, Luke takes Theophilus through Jesus' career in order to review how God worked to legitimize Jesus and how Jesus proclaimed hope . . . The offer of the Gospel openly includes Theophilus and calls him to remain faithful, committed, and expectant, even in the midst of intense Jewish rejection and with the hope that both Jews and Gentiles will return to Jesus.[16]

Certainly there were many others who shared Theophilus's struggle, and on the assumption that Luke knew their struggles too, we therefore can very well understand that Luke would have wished for his Gospel to reach a wider readership. Song captured this thought when he wrote, "Luke's purpose is to show the Gentile Christians on what firm historic facts their faith is based."[17] But Luke's purpose cannot be restricted to this alone and Song acknowledges this: "Luke relates the historical events and words of his Gospel not merely for the sake of historical writing. He wrote with the object of convincing, converting, saving, and spiritually edifying his fellowmen."[18]

Luke's Gospel is the longest book in the NT, and the combined Luke-Acts comprises more than one quarter of the NT. Based on the NA[28], Luke has 1,151 verses compared to Matthew's 1,071, Mark's 678, and John's 869. Luke's basic outline of Jesus' ministry resembles that of Matthew and Mark: preparation period, ministry in Galilee, movement to Jerusalem, and then passion and resurrection. But Luke differs on many crucial points. For instance, he devotes ten chapters (9:51—19:27) to the account of Jesus' movement to Jerusalem, whereas Matthew allots only two (19-20) and Mark one (10) to the same topic. He shrinks his account of Jesus' ministry in Galilee to 4:14—9:17, much shorter compared to Matthew's 4:12—16:12 and Mark's 1:14—8:26.

He also reports certain details that are not shared by the other Gospels, namely the parables of the Good Samaritan (10:25–37), the Prodigal

16. Bock, *Luke*, 1:15.
17. Song, "Exodus," 6.
18. Song, "Exodus," 6.

Son (15:11–32), and the Shrewd Manager (16:1–9), the report of Jesus' encounter with Zacchaeus (19:1–10), Jesus' raising of a widow's son at Nain (7:11–17), and Jesus' prayer on the cross asking God to forgive his executioners (23:34) and assuring the believing thief beside him of entrance into Paradise (23:43). All these observations heighten the fact that Luke was both a historian and a theologian. As Marshall explains,

> Luke's theology is closely related to that of his sources . . . [He] wished to give a faithful portrayal of the ministry of Jesus and the life of the early church. He did not, therefore, write a work of creative imagination, but was very much controlled by his sources. He believed that the Christian faith rested upon the events associated with the work of Jesus and the apostles, and so he gave a historical (not a "historicizing") account of what had happened in order to confirm the faith of his readers.[19]

What are the key themes and emphases of Luke-Acts? First, God's plan is very much emphasized and highlighted. For example, we see in Luke's infancy narratives that he intends not only to connect Jesus' life and ministry to Israel's story in the OT but also to present Jesus as the fulfillment of God's promises in the OT (1:54–55, 68–79; 2:29–32; cf. Jesus' declaration in 4:18–19). Luke's frequent use of δεῖ ("it is necessary") suggests the same point. He has Jesus declare in 24:44, "Everything written about me in the law of Moses, the prophets, and the psalms must [δεῖ] be fulfilled." For Luke, therefore, Jesus—his birth, death, and resurrection—was not a fluke or an accident. In Jesus, God's promises to Israel were fulfilled. And that relates to the second theme—God's plan of offering salvation for the world through Jesus.

The centrality of the notion of salvation in Luke is evidenced by the fact that he is the only synoptic evangelist who uses the noun "salvation,"[20] and he employs the verb "save" (σῴζω) more than any other NT book. In Luke 19:10, after Zacchaeus's conversion, Jesus said, "For the Son of Man came to seek and to save the lost." Salvation is the key concept in Luke's theology, where

> it refers to the content of the good news preached by Jesus, a message which brought men and women deliverance from their sin and the joy of the kingdom of God. In the preaching of the apostles

---

19. Marshall, *Luke*, 9.

20. Σωτηρία four times (1:69, 71, 77; 19:9), σωτήριον twice (2:30; 3:6), and σωτήρ also twice (1:47; 2:11).

it comprised the offer of forgiveness of sins and the gift of the Holy Spirit. Salvation was thus a present possession, whose reality was known by those who repented and believed in Jesus Christ, but at the same time it was a foretaste of the future blessings associated with His parousia.[21]

The third theme is related to the first two. Luke emphasizes the Gentiles as also God-intended recipients of God's salvation. The universal scope of God's plan of salvation is hinted early in Luke with his tracing Jesus' genealogy all the way back to Adam (as distinct from Matthew's Abraham). In Luke 4:25–27, Jesus rebukes the people and reminds them of God's grace for the widow of Zarephath and Naaman of Syria. In 7:1–10, Jesus praises a Gentile centurion for his faith. In 10:30–37, in the very famous parable, Jesus makes a Samaritan the hero, not the Levite or the Jewish priest.

Finally, the fourth theme is Luke's emphasis on Jesus' concern for the outcasts of society. He presents Jesus as always interacting with those rejected by Jewish mainstream society: the poor (1:46–55; 4:18; 6:20–23; 7:22; 10:21–22; 14:13, 21–24; 16:19–31; 21:1–4), "sinners" (5:27–32; 7:28, 30, 34, 36–50; 15:1–2; 19:7), and women (7:36–50; 8:1–3, 48; 10:38–42; 13:10–17; 24:1–12). These outcasts are pictured by Luke as particularly responsive to Jesus' message.[22]

The flow of Luke's narrative can be smoothly traced and outlined by identifying the key geographical areas of action. Applying this principle, Luke's basic outline will not differ from Mark's:

Location	Luke's Textual Division	Heading
	1:1–4	Prologue
	1:5–2:52	The birth of John the Baptist and the birth of Jesus
Galilee	3:1–4:13	Jesus' preparation for the ministry
	4:14–9:50	Jesus' ministry in Galilee
On the road from Galilee to Jerusalem	9:51–19:44	Jesus' transition from Galilee to Jerusalem

---

21. Marshall, *Luke*, 9.
22. Carson and Moo, *Introduction*, 219–21.

| Jerusalem | 19:45–21:38 | Jesus' ministry in Jerusalem |
| | 22:1–24:53 | Jesus' crucifixion and resurrection |

The Immediate Contexts of the Temple Incident

Let us now analyze the immediate contexts of the temple incident pericope: Jesus' entry into Jerusalem (19:28–40), his lament over Jerusalem (19:41–44), and his daily teaching at the temple (19:47–48).

Jesus' Entry into Jerusalem (19:28–40)

Here is Luke's account of Jesus' entry into Jerusalem:

> 28 After he had said this, he went on ahead, going up to Jerusalem. 29 When he had come near Bethphage and Bethany, at the place called the Mount of Olives, he sent two of the disciples, 30 saying, "Go into the village ahead of you, and as you enter it you will find tied there a colt that has never been ridden. Untie it and bring it here. 31 If anyone asks you, "Why are you untying it?" just say this, "The Lord needs it." 32 So those who were sent departed and found it as he had told them. 33 As they were untying the colt, its owners asked them, "Why are you untying the colt?" 34 They said, "The Lord needs of it." 35 Then they brought it to Jesus; and after throwing their cloaks on the colt, they set Jesus on it. 36 As he rode along, people kept spreading their cloaks on the road. 37 As he was now approaching the path down from the Mount of Olives, the whole multitude of the disciples began to praise God joyfully with a loud voice for all the deeds of power that they had seen, 38 saying, "Blessed is the king who comes in the name of the Lord! Peace in heaven and glory in the highest heaven!" 39 Some of the Pharisees in the crowd said to him, "Teacher, rebuke your disciples." 40 He answered, "I tell you, if these were silent, the stones would shout out."

It is helpful to quickly review here the material that Luke shares in common with Matthew and Mark. First, common to all three synoptic Gospels is the reference to Jesus' going up to Jerusalem. Second, in common with Mark, Luke mentions "Bethphage and Bethany at the Mount of Olives," whereas

Matthew mentions only "Bethany at the Mount of Olives." Third, common to all three Gospels is the report about Jesus sending two disciples, and now Luke together with Mark says that the two disciples were to fetch "a colt," whereas Matthew says "a donkey and her colt." Fourth, Luke and Mark describe the colt as "unridden." Fifth, all the three report that the two disciples went and did exactly as Jesus had told them. For Luke and Mark, the two disciples untied the colt and brought it to Jesus. For Matthew, there were two animals: "the donkey and her colt." Sixth, all three report that the disciples (most probably the same two disciples) "put their cloaks on the animal" (except that in Matthew there are two animals). Seventh, all tree report of the crowd's putting their cloaks on the road ahead of Jesus (Luke omits reference to cut-out leaves). Eighth, all three refer to a big group of people accompanying Jesus. Ninth, Luke shares with Matthew and Mark the phrase εὐλογημένος ὁ ἐρχόμενος . . . ἐν ὀνόματι κυρίου ("blessed is the one . . . who comes in the name of the Lord") and ἐν ὑψίστοις ("in the highest").

Unique to Luke are the following details: (1) the reference to the colt's οἱ κύριοι ("owners") in verse 32; (2) whereas Matthew and Mark say that "Jesus sat on the colt" (again, Matthew has two animals in mind), Luke reports that "the disciples set Jesus on it" (v. 35b); (3) verse 37, except the reference to the multitude, is unparalleled in Matthew and Mark (the key elements are: "down from the Mount of Olives," the emphasis on the "whole multitude praising God joyfully" (Matthew and Mark do not mention God), and "the deeds of power that the multitude had seen"); (4) ὁ βασιλεὺς ("the King") in Luke 19:38 is unparalleled; Mark has ἡ ἐρχομένη βασιλεία ("the coming kingdom"); (5) ἐν οὐρανῷ εἰρήνη καὶ δόξα ("in [the] heavens peace and glory") is unique to Luke; and (6) verses 39 and 40, καί τινες τῶν Φαρισαίων ἀπὸ τοῦ ὄχλου εἶπαν πρὸς αὐτόν, Διδάσκαλε, ἐπιτίμησον τοῖς μαθηταῖς σου. καὶ ἀποκριθεὶς εἶπεν, Λέγω ὑμῖν, ἐὰν οὗτοι σιωπήσουσιν, οἱ λίθοι κράξουσιν ("And some of the Pharisees in the multitude said to him, "Teacher, rebuke your disciples." He answered, "I tell you, if these were silent, the very stones would cry out.").

Comparing Luke's to Matthew's and Mark's accounts, we see the following notable omissions: (1) καὶ εὐθὺς αὐτὸν ἀποστέλλει πάλιν ὧδε ("and he will send it back here immediately"); (2) στιβάδας κόψαντες ἐκ τῶν ἀγρῶν ("leaves cut out from the fields"); (3) Ὡσαννά ("Hosanna"); and (4) the reference to David's name.

Key Emphases of Luke's Account of Jesus' Entry into Jerusalem

Based on the common details shared by Luke with the other evangelists, we can expect that Luke also shares with them specific themes and emphases about the main character of this episode, Jesus.

Jesus' Royalty or Kingship

In fact, Luke has emphasized Jesus' kingship more strongly than has Mark. Let us analyze Luke's report. First, in common with the other evangelists, there is Luke's presentation of Jesus' entering Jerusalem not on foot but riding on a colt. Luke's account conveys Jesus' intentionality, purposefulness, and preparation, and it is not difficult to detect that Jesus was into something here, that not only was he aware of who he is—as the Messiah and a Davidic royal[23]—but also that he was intent on disclosing his identity, through his symbolic gestures here, to Jerusalem. In fact, he was here presenting himself to Jerusalem as her Messiah and King. Jesus' entry into Jerusalem, with all its accompanying details, ought to be viewed as his prophetic, symbolic action (as I have argued elsewhere in this work).

Second, notice how Luke begins his report: "When he had said this" (19:28). This comment significantly links the account of Jesus' entry into Jerusalem (19:28-40) to the previous passage which is the parable of the "rejected king" (11:11-27) in which Jesus is "implicitly identified as the nobleman."[24]

Third, Luke's explanatory note (shared by Mark but not Matthew) that the colt was "unridden" also lends support to his emphasis on Jesus' royalty. This is of course a Jewish convention (see Num 19:2; Deut 21:3; 1 Sam 6:7; 2 Sam 6:3): animals for sacred or royal use should be set aside only for such purposes.[25] An unridden colt fits well Jesus' sacred and royal dignity.[26]

Fourth, the distinctly Lucan οἱ κύριοι (v. 33) parallels the ὁ κύριος of verse 34, which here refers to Jesus.[27] Notice what Luke is trying to say.

---

23. For Strauss (*Messiah*, 306), Luke actually reiterates Jesus' royal status in three keys passages: the account of the blind man outside Jericho (18:35–43), the parable of the pounds (19:11–27), and the triumphal entry (19:28–40).

24. Chanikuzhy, *Jesus*, 116; cf. Kinman, *Entry*, 91; Kinman, "Parousia."

25. Marshall, *Luke*, 712.

26. So Nolland, *Luke*, 924–25.

27. So Danker, *Jesus*, 312; Liefeld, "Luke," 1011.

When Jesus' two disciples untie the colt, its owners questioned them about why they are untying it, and then they respond by saying, "The Lord, or the 'Owner,' needs it." Jesus, the ultimate Owner of all things, deserves the ultimate rights to all our possessions, for we are only contingent owners.

Fifth, another salient indication of Lucan emphasis on Jesus' kingship is Luke's unparalleled comment, saying that the disciples "put Jesus on the colt" (Matthew and Mark indicate that Jesus mounts the colt by himself). Drumann[28] finds a connection to how Solomon was set on a mule according to the command of David (1 Kgs 1:33). Finally, there is Luke's addition of ὁ βασιλεὺς to his quotation of Ps 118:26 as the acclamation of the jubilant crowd (this is uniquely Luke's detail). The result is this: "Blessed is *the King* who comes in the name of the Lord! Peace in heaven and glory in the highest heaven!" (Luke 19:38). Compare this with, for example, Mark 11:9, "Hosanna! Blessed is he who comes in the name of the Lord!" We recall that Luke earlier alludes to Jesus' kingship in 1:32 and 18:38–39 (cf. 23:3, 37–38; Acts 17:7).

Jesus' Messiahship

This is of course not uniquely Lucan, for all the other evangelists were also very eager to present that Jesus entered Jerusalem as the Messiah. The usual supports are the same. Jesus' riding into the city mounting a colt is itself a messianic image, alluding to Zech 9 where the prophet foretells the coming into Jerusalem of the Messiah-King. Particularly Zechariah pictures the Messiah-King riding on a colt (the LXX mentions a "new colt") into Jerusalem (Zech 9:9–10). So Luke, as do the other evangelists, presents Jesus here as the Messiah entering Jerusalem according to the prophecy of Zechariah. That is, Jesus by his actions here has fulfilled prophecy.

Another indication of Lucan emphasis on Jesus' messiahship is his not mentioning that Jesus "entered into Jerusalem"; instead, Luke tells us that Jesus entered the temple! This tends to indicate that Luke did not care so much about Jerusalem as Jesus' destination. Perhaps so, and Luke might have had in mind really the temple as Jesus' final destination. This is significant, for it indicates fulfillment of Malachi 3:1, which says that the Lord will suddenly come to his temple.[29]

---

28. As cited in Chanikuzhy, *Jesus*, 117.
29. So Fitzmyer, *Gospel*, 2:1251.

Thirdly, as do the other synoptic evangelists, Luke describes Jesus as ὁ ἐρχόμενος ("the one who is coming" or "the coming one"). This is a messianic expression.[30] We recall that in Luke 7:20 Jesus was asked whether he was "the coming one." Here in Luke 19:38, the crowd of disciples (a distinctly Lucan expression) answers that question with a resounding "yes."[31]

Contrasting Responses to Jesus

Jesus' presentation and offering of himself as the Messiah-King through his highly symbolic gestures was a highly polarizing act, and Luke portrays this reality more strongly than do the other evangelists. On the one hand, we see the enthusiastic response of the multitude whom Luke describes as Jesus' disciples (v. 37). The other evangelists also report about the crowd that accompanied Jesus, but unlike Luke they did not reckon them as Jesus' disciples.

Next, Luke says that the multitude of Jesus' disciples acknowledge him as "the King," "the coming one." On the other hand, we also see the unbelieving response of the Pharisees, which Luke specifically describes as being "in the crowd." This is also unparalleled in the other Gospels. There were bad eggs in the crowd—the Pharisees! They said to Jesus, "Teacher, rebuke your disciples." Many interpretations have been put forth as to why these Pharisees made this request.[32] Stein's comment is right: these Pharisees wanted "to squelch the disciples' praise of God."[33] They did not agree with the content of the crowd's acclamation, which is equal to, they did not regard Jesus as the Messiah-King, though they regarded him as "rabbi." Of course, this unbelief and resistance betokens what Jesus would encounter later in Jerusalem—rejection, opposition, and scheming by the chief priests, elders, and scribes.

---

30. So Ellis, *Gospel*, 227.
31. So Danker, *Jesus*, 313.
32. Bock, *Luke*, 2:1559–60, for a list of these interpretations.
33. Stein, *Luke*, 481.

The Fulfillment of God's Plan—The Coming of Hope for Israel and the World

This theme overlaps with the first and second emphases discussed above. We read in Luke 19:37: "the whole multitude of the disciples began to praise God joyfully with a loud voice for all the deeds of power that they had seen." Note the mention of "deeds of power." Notice further that the crowd saw these mighty works themselves, and now they are praising and giving glory to God. What are these mighty works? The Lucan corpus (Luke-Acts) frequently tells us about Jesus' miraculous deeds, and Luke is careful to note that people who experienced such miraculous acts ended up praising God or putting their faith in him (5:25–26; 7:16; 13:13; 17:15, 18; 18:43; 19:37). Tannehill explains, "Jesus' mighty acts are signs that God is at work to bring about the fulfillment of a comprehensive hope for Israel and the world, long planned and long prophesied in Scripture."[34] The multitude understood that not only has the kingdom come, the King himself has come! Hence, it goes back to one of Luke's themes discussed above, that Luke presents Jesus' life, ministry, death, and resurrection not only as the fulfillment of God's promises of old but also that through and in Jesus the whole world will receive God's blessing.

Jesus' Lament over Jerusalem (19:41–44)

The account of Jesus' weeping for Jerusalem is distinctly Lucan. Here is the NRSV rendition of Luke 19:41–44:

> 41 And when he drew near and saw the city he wept over it, 42 saying, "Would that even today you knew the things that make for peace! But now they are hid from your eyes. 43 For the days shall come upon you, when your enemies will cast up a bank about you and surround you, and hem you in on every side, 44 and dash you to the ground, you and your children within you, and they will not leave one stone upon another in you; because you did not know the time of your visitation."

Two things in this passage should occupy our attention. First is the fact that Jesus' wept (vv. 41–42). Why did he weep? What are its implications? Second is the content of Jesus' prophetic pronouncement (vv. 43–44).

---

34. Tannehill, *Luke*, 87.

Luke tells us that Jesus wept as soon as he saw the city. It is only in this passage and in John 11:35 where we read of Jesus' weeping. This was not of course tears of joy, but of divine sorrow, as verse 42 makes clear: "If you, even you, had only recognized on this day the things that make for peace! But now they are hidden from your eyes." Fitzmyer has paraphrased this verse thus, "It would have pleased me if you had known the things that made for peace."[35] Jesus' weeping was occasioned by two things of "cause-and-effect" relationship. Jesus wept because of Jerusalem's rejection of him. Jerusalem did not know what would bring her peace (quite ironic since her name meant peace, "*salem*"). Evans writes, with a pun, "Jesus laments ironically that the city of peace does not know what to do in order to secure peace."[36] This peace is of course a summative word for the gospel[37] or salvation.[38] Jerusalem's ignorance, unbelief, and rejection of her Royal Messiah incurred her own doom. Knowing the cataclysmic judgment that awaited the city, Jesus wept, an action that has prophetic parallels in Jeremiah's weeping (Jer 9:2 [9:1 MT]; 13:17; 14:7; cf. 2 Kgs 8:11; Gen 50:1; Num 11:13; Judg 11:37–38).

Next we consider Jesus' "oracle of doom"[39] for Jerusalem (vv. 43–44). We note first of all that this is the second time in Luke that Jesus prophesies against the city, the first time in 13:34–35 and the third in 23:26–31. Second, this is a prophecy, not a *vaticinium ex eventu* ("post-event prediction"), which was fulfilled in the fall of Jerusalem in the hands of the Romans in 70 CE.[40] Third, the language of this prophecy is derived from OT prophetic passages that had to do with the first destruction of Jerusalem and the first temple.[41] Three terms in particular—χάραξ, κύκλος, and συνέχειν—come from Jeremiah's description of the Babylonian siege on Jerusalem (Jer 52:4f); "the razing of town and children" come from Ps 136:9 LXX. The Romans' not leaving one stone upon another is from Jesus' own words in Mark 13:2 (par. Luke 21:6).[42]

---

35. Fitzmyer, *Gospel*, 2:1258.
36. Evans, *Luke*, 290.
37. Bock, *Luke*, 2:1560.
38. Marshall, *Gospel*, 718.
39. Thiede, *Prophecy*, 80.
40. In this book I support a pre-70 CE dating for the composition of Luke's Gospel.
41. Evans, *Luke*, 290.
42. Goulder, *Luke*, 689.

To sum up, like no other Gospel writer, Luke has shown us the impact of Jerusalem's ignorance, opposition to, and rejection of her Messiah-King. Jesus wept over the city, an occurrence that had prophetic parallels in the past. Jesus wept not only because the city rejected his claims but also because, as a result of that rejection, she was destined for God's judgment in the hands of the Romans, just as the Judah of old was also destroyed at the hands of the Babylonians. Luke 19:41–44 anticipates the conflict that would further play out in subsequent Lucan chapters.

Jesus' Daily Teaching at the Temple (19:47–48)

Our final contextual consideration is Jesus' daily teaching at the temple (vv. 47–48), which took place after Jesus' temple act. Here is the NRSV's rendition:

> 47 Every day he was teaching in the temple. The chief priests, the scribes, and the leaders of the people kept looking for a way to kill him; 48 but they did not find anything they could do, for all the people were spellbound by what they heard.

The place of action is now inside the temple, at the temple precincts, which is a very large area. Luke tells us in verse 47 that Jesus was teaching daily in the temple. This was Passover week, so we can be certain that this daily teaching did not last for the whole week, for we know that Jesus would soon be arrested, tried and crucified. What we know from Mark's account is that Jesus traveled daily in and out of the city. He would be in Jerusalem in the daytime and back in Bethany at night. But certainly Luke's focus here is on Jesus' teaching which occasioned the Sanhedrin's seeking to destroy him. In Mark's account, it was also Jesus' teaching combined with his demonstration at the temple precincts that provoked the Sanhedrin to plot against him. That is also what Luke tells us here. Luke also tells us that the crowd "hung on to Jesus' words," which made it difficult for the Sanhedrin to kill him.

In sum, Luke is giving much emphasis on Jesus' teaching as one serious reason for the Jewish leaders to want to kill him. This observation has an important implication for our understanding of Jesus' temple act in Luke, to which we are turning next.

ANALYSIS OF THE TEMPLE INCIDENT IN LUKE 19:45–46[43]

Greek text:

> 45 Καὶ εἰσελθὼν εἰς τὸ ἱερὸν ἤρξατο ἐκβάλλειν τοὺς πωλοῦντας, 46 λέγων αὐτοῖς, Γέγραπται, Καὶ ἔσται ὁ οἶκός μου οἶκος προσευχῆς, ὑμεῖς δὲ αὐτὸν ἐποιήσατε σπήλαιον λῃστῶν.

My own translation:

> 45 And after entering the temple, he began to drive out those who sold, 46 saying to them, "It is written, 'My house shall be a house of prayer'; but you have made it a den of robbers."

Analysis

What is immediately striking is the brevity of Luke's account compared to the other evangelists' (this becomes more striking when we consider the fact that Luke is the longest Gospel). Luke has left out so many details that the other Gospels have carefully included. This observation immediately raises questions of intents on Luke's part for not reporting this or that detail, and these questions are perfectly valid in light of the well-established understanding that the evangelists were not only historians but also theologians who had certain purposes for the way they composed their respective Gospels.

What details did Luke retain? (Appendix 1 will help to spot the parallels and discontinuities). Luke reports the following and it may helpful to breakdown the component parts of verses 45 and 46: (1) the reference to "having come into" or "entered" the temple (καὶ εἰσελθὼν εἰς τὸ ἱερόν); (2) there is reference to Jesus' "starting" (ἤρξατο) the action—his protest; (3) Luke uses the same verb for Jesus' action—he "drove out" of the temple those who were selling there (ἐκβάλλειν τοὺς πωλοῦντας, and here Luke stops short of the other Gospels' reporting); (4) there is reference to Jesus' "speaking to the people" (λέγων αὐτοῖς), resembling Matthew but not Mark who adds the idea of Jesus' teaching (Luke's reference to Jesus' teaching daily in the temple follows the temple incident, 19:47–48); (5) the quote

---

43. Refer to Appendix 2 for a color-coded comparison of the Synoptic Gospels' accounts of the temple incident.

from Isa 56 is included, though excluding the phrase "for all the nations"; and (6) the quote from Jer 7 is included intact.

We can identify the following distinctives of Luke's account:[44] (1) Luke has a significantly shorter account: sixty-one words versus Mark's eighty-nine; (2) Luke lacks the temporal markers of Mark 11:12 that reveal that the event took place on the day after Jesus' entry (i.e., on a Tuesday). In Luke, Jesus goes directly into the temple; (3) Luke omits reference to the fig tree's withering (Mark 11:12–14 = Matt 21:18– 19); (4) Luke does not detail any violent acts, such as the use of a whip (John 2:15) or the overturning of tables (Mark 11:15); (5) Luke does not mention that Jesus blocked people's way into the court (Mark 11:16); and (6) Luke does not mention that the temple is a place for the nations (Mark 11:17).

Themes and Emphases

Based on the little that Luke has said and on the much that he has left out (based of course on our wholistic knowledge of this incident drawn from the other Gospels), we can identify the following Lucan emphases and priorities.

Jesus' Kingship and Messiahship

Despite the brevity of the account, Luke's emphasis on Jesus' kingship and messiahship is still evident. This is of course a carry-over from the previous event, which is Jesus' entry into the city. Very clearly—through Jesus' well-orchestrated actions and the multitude's acclamation—Luke presents Jesus as coming to Jerusalem as the royal Messiah. But surprisingly Luke does not mention that Jesus entered the city, instead, he makes reference to Jesus' entering the temple! And it is as such, as the royal Messiah, that Jesus enters God's house. "Jesus' visit to the Temple takes on the character of the expected appearance of the Lord in his house on his day," Dawsey writes.[45] Despite all the details that Luke leaves out, he tells us that Jesus drove out all the sellers. Parallel to the other Gospels, Luke has Jesus legitimize his action by quoting from Isa 56:7, "My house shall be called a house of prayer" (Luke leaves out the phrase "for all the nations"), and from Jer 7:11, but you

---

44. See Bock, *Luke*, 2:1574; Fitzmyer, *Luke*, 2:1261.
45. Dawsey, "Confrontation," 157.

have made it "a den of robbers." Rahner suggests that by the phrase λέγων αὐτοῖς in 19:46 (instead of the Markan interrogative form καὶ ἐδίδασκεν καὶ ἔλεγεν αὐτοῖς, Οὐ γέγραπται) Luke links Jesus' scriptural quotations in 19:46 directly to his action in 19:45, in which case Jesus' action loses force and is dominated by Jesus' scriptural quotations.[46]

The Temple

First, we want to understand why Luke excluded the phrase πᾶσιν τοῖς ἔθνεσιν, particularly in consideration of Luke's emphasis on the universality of God's saving plan. Marshall answers this by saying that Luke in the first place was aware that the temple did not become a "house of prayer for all nations."[47] Marshall is here of course referring to the fact that later on this temple would be utterly destroyed. This explanation is reasonable and it could well have been Luke's reason for excluding the phrase. Another equally likely explanation is to point out to what the temple had become in Jesus' time. That is, God's intent was for it to be a house of prayer for all nations, but the Jewish leaders had turned it into a den of thieves. Considering this sad state of the temple, Luke left out the phrase.

Second, let us inquire into the implication of the brevity of Luke's account on his views on the temple. This strange brevity has led Marshall to suggest that this incident has no deeper significance for Luke.[48] This suggestion may seem reasonable on the surface, but not when we begin to realize that the shortness of this account is purposeful on Luke's part. Then, what was Luke's purpose in radically shortening his report, excluding references to Jesus' seemingly "violent" acts? Kinman has proposed that Luke did not wish his readers to mistake Jesus for a Jewish nationalist rebel against Rome.[49] Kinman points out that Jewish nationalist rebels were known for their zeal for the Jerusalem temple and so historically the temple had become a hatching ground for their revolutionary campaign against Rome. Josephus, for example, tells us that at one time, Archelaus sent his army to squelch a rebellion in the temple, killing three thousand rebels (*A. J.* 17.213–218). Kinman's suggestion may look reasonable, but not when we

---

46. Cited in Chanikuzhy, *Jesus*, 223.
47. Marshall, *Gospel*, 721.
48. Marshall, *Gospel*, 721.
49. Kinman, *Entry*, 154–55.

consider the other Gospels' accounts, which are longer and detailed and yet do not give the impression that Jesus was acting like an anti-Roman rebel.

Obviously, the explanation for Luke's strangely short account lies somewhere else, and there are ready clues in Luke's extended narrative that will help us to locate the answer. One such clue is Luke's obviously purposeful decision of not mentioning Jesus' entrance into Jerusalem (Luke leaves the reader to deduce it from context); instead, he mentions Jesus entering the temple. This clue indicates that in Luke's narrative the temple plays a more significant role than does Jerusalem. The second clue is Luke's leaving out references to Jesus' "violent" acts: overturning the tables of the money-changers and the seats of the dove-sellers (Matthew, Mark, and John) and prohibiting any one to carry any goods across or through the temple (Mark). The third and final clue is Luke's reference to Jesus' daily teaching in the temple (19:47, καὶ ἦν διδάσκων τὸ καθ' ἡμέραν ἐν τῷ ἱερῷ). All these clues point to a distinct role that Luke has assigned to Jesus' temple act in the Lucan narrative.

It is good to remind ourselves that "the temple functions as a key [geographical] location in Luke"[50] and that also it "functions as the *literary center* of Luke-Acts."[51] Weinert asserts that the theme of "the role of the Temple in Luke-Acts is widely recognized by commentators as a prominent motif in Luke's work."[52] In addition to all this, we should also note, as Weinert has demonstrated, that Luke displays a positive outlook towards the temple.[53] According to Nolland, Luke's "severe abbreviation" of the account is due to his concern "to minimize any sense in which Jesus might be seen as critical of the Jerusalem temple."[54]

SUMMARY AND CONCLUSION

What is the role of Jesus' temple act in the Lucan narrative? It is not true that Luke's strange brevity speaks of purposelessness or that this incident is unimportant to him. In fact, Luke's choice to leave out many details that the other Gospels included speaks a lot about his view of the temple and indicates the function of the temple incident in his narrative. We have seen

50. Fay, "Temple," 258, emphasis added.
51. Fay, "Temple," 255, italics added.
52. Weinert, "Luke," 68.
53. Weinert, "Meaning,"; Weinert, "Luke, Stephen."
54. Nolland, *Luke*, 937.

that Luke portrays a positive outlook towards the temple. This is most likely the reason why he did not report on Jesus' seemingly violent acts in the temple— such as overturning tables and chairs, using a whip to drive out animals, and blockading the temple precincts from passers-by who brought goods. Luke's report in 19:47 that Jesus subsequently taught *daily* in the temple points to a positive meaning of Jesus' temple act: He "cleansed" the temple by driving out the sellers in order to reclaim it and prepare it as a place for his teaching ministry.[55] Weinert adds, "For Luke, the temple of Jesus' time remains God's 'house' by prophetic and scriptural standards (19:46; cf. Isa 56:7). It is a valid, proper place of prayer in Israel, which Jesus affirms but does not threaten to replace."[56] Chance writes, "The Messiah restores the temple, rendering it fit to fulfill its eschatological role as a decisive center of God's saving work."[57]

The Lucan community would have easily seen and understood Luke's high regard for the Jewish temple. They could not have otherwise missed it because right at the beginning of the Gospel, Luke tells the stories of his Gospel's two key personalities—John the Baptist and Jesus—and locates those stories right at the Jerusalem temple. It was in the context of priest Zechariah's service in the temple when an angel of the Lord unveiled to him that his wife would conceive a baby, and we know that baby to be John the Baptist (1:5–25). Luke 2 tells two stories of Jesus, both happening in the temple: baby Jesus' presentation to the Lord (2:21–40) and the twelve-year-old Jesus engaging with teachers. What is more, Luke's last verse (24:53) centers on the temple: "And they [the disciples] stayed continually at the temple, praising God." So when Theophilus and the rest of Luke's readers perused the pericope of Jesus' temple act, they would have understood it without difficulty as meaning Jesus' "cleansing" and reclaiming the temple for his purposes, specifically as "a house of prayer" and a site for his teaching ministry. To convey that, Luke only devoted two verses to Jesus' temple action (19:45–46), limiting his reference to Jesus driving out the sellers and his statement, "'My house will be a house of prayer,' but you have made it 'a den of robbers.'" To include other details would detract from his purposes.

---

55. See Conzelmann, *Theology*, 77.
56. Weinert, "Luke," 71.
57. Chance, *Jerusalem*, 57–58.

5

The Significance of the Johannine Temple Incident

CONTEXTUAL CONSIDERATIONS

THE GOAL OF THIS chapter is to grasp the significance of the Johannine temple incident (2:13–22) using a compositional analysis. As in the previous chapters, the discussion here will proceed in three steps. First, we will attempt to grasp the big picture of John's Gospel. What is this Gospel about? Why was it written? What are its themes and key emphases? Second, we will consider the immediate contexts of the Johannine temple incident, namely the miracle of turning water to wine in 2:1–11 and the summative statement of unbelief in 2:23–25. Then, third, we will focus on the Johannine temple incident and determine its distinctive meaning and significance.[1]

John's Authorship, Overall Message, and Emphases

The authorship of John's Gospel remains a contested question in scholarship. Like the Synoptic Gospels, John did not originally bear its author's name. As many scholars have pointed out,[2] the four canonical Gospels were

---

1. Refer to Appendix 1 for a comparison of the contextual location of Jesus' temple act in the Gospels.

2. E.g., Porter and Pitts, *Origins*, 439; Köstenberger and Patterson, *Interpretation*,

formally anonymous (they do not identify their authors) and the attribution of their authorship to specific individuals owes itself to the act of the early church at the time when the four Gospels were first bound together and circulated as one collective document. What prompted the identification of author was probably convenience in distinguishing one Gospel from another. "According to John" or whatever form it was originally may have from there on served as John's working title.[3]

Majority of critical scholars reject Johannine (apostolic) authorship. Many espouse the view that the Gospel was produced by the so-called Johannine school or community.[4] Among conservative and moderate scholars, two views have been advanced. Some argue that the Gospel was written by John the apostle,[5] while others claim that it was written by John the Elder.[6]

In the midst of these scholarly debates, and in spite of them, the testimony of ancient Christian writers should not be disregarded but should be given due consideration. Many contemporary scholars have investigated and analyzed the external evidence, and the uniform conclusion has been that the early church unanimously upheld Johannine (apostolic) authorship of the Gospel.[7]

We may correlate this external evidence with a piece of internal evidence; that is, the probable identity of "the disciple whom Jesus loved" (henceforth "Beloved Disciple") who first explicitly appears at the Last Supper, described in 13:23 as reclining next to Jesus. The Synoptics tell us that only the apostles (the Twelve) participated in the Supper.[8] We may adduce

---

371-72.

3. Martin Hengel (*The Johannine Question*) has vigorously challenged the view that the Gospels were formally anonymous. He has argued that the Gospels were not anonymous from the very beginning, for it was simply inconceivable for them to circulate anonymously for decades and later attain identity of authorship.

4. See, e.g., Cullmann, *Johannine Circle*; Brown, *Community*; Culpepper, *Johannine School*.

5. Supported by such scholars as Carson, *Gospel*, 68-81; Bruce, *Gospel*; Blomberg, *Reliability*; Milne, *Message*.

6. Martin Hengel has devoted an entire monograph (*The Johannine Question*) to advancing the view that the beloved disciple, credited by the Gospel itself as its author, was John the Elder (not John the apostle). This view is followed and defended by Richard Bauckham in many of his publications: e.g., "Papias"; "Eyewitness"; "Beloved Disciple."

7. Blomberg, *Reliability*, 22-40; Keener, *Gospel*, 1:91-104; Carson and Moo, *Introduction*, 229-35; Carson, *Gospel*, 68-81; Morris, *Gospel*, 21-30.

8. See Matt 26:20; Mark 14:17; Luke 22:14.

from this that the Beloved Disciple was one of the Twelve. Morever, based on many passages in John[9] we can infer that the Beloved Disciple is not Peter and not any one of the apostles named in chapters 13–16. Furthermore, John 21 tells us that he is one of the seven who went fishing, which means that he is not Peter, Thomas, or Nathanael, and that he must be one of the two sons of Zebedee, or one of the other two disciples referred to in 21:2. He cannot be James because as we know James died early by martyrdom, perhaps within 41–44 CE. Furthermore, the Fourth Gospel very strangely indeed does not refer to James or John by name, whereas it names the other apostles including the less prominent ones like Philip and Judas. Whereas the Synoptics frequently picture Peter in the company of John son of Zebedee,[10] the Fourth Gospel does not. It assigns specific names to key characters—Simon Peter, Thomas Didymus, Judas son of Simon Iscariot, Caiaphas, the high priest that year—but it is strange when this Gospel calls John the Baptist by only the short form "John." All these textual data and observations do seem to point to the expected conclusion that the Beloved Disciple, to whose authorship the Fourth Gospel was attributed, was none other than John the son of Zebedee.[11]

Various dates have been assigned to John, ranging from before the fall of Jerusalem (70 CE) to the last quarter of the second century. But the discovery in 1920 of the papyrus P^{52} (a small fragment containing John 18:31–33, 37–38),[12] dated to the early part of the second century CE and arguably the earliest known fragment of the NT, narrows our options, eliminating very late dates, leaving us with two options: a date before 70 CE[13] or a date towards the close of the first century (80–85 CE,[14] 80 CE,[15] or mid-90s CE[16]). The internal evidence does not clearly indicate the date, so we are left with the witness of ancient church tradition, which favors any date from the 80s to the 90s. This is the general position taken in this book.

---

9. See, e.g., 13:23–24; 20:2–9; 21:20.

10. E.g., Mark 5:37; 9:2; 14:33 and Acts 3:1–4:23; 8:15–25.

11. For a substantial defense of the identification of the Beloved Disciple as John the son of Zebedee, see Köstenberger, "Disciple Jesus Loved."

12. See Blomberg, *Reliability*, 31–41 for further discussion.

13. Robinson, *Redating*, 310–11; Morris, *Gospel*, 34.

14. Carson and Moo, *Introduction*, 267.

15. Carson, *Gospel*, 82. Carson admits, however, that "none of the arguments is entirely convincing, and almost any date between AD 55 and AD 95 is possible."

16. Keener, *Gospel*, 1:140.

John tells us his purpose for writing: "Now Jesus did many other signs in the presence of his disciples, which are not written in this book. But these are written so that you may believe that Jesus is the Messiah, the Son of God, and that through believing you may have life in his name" (20:30–31). Although this purpose appears plain and straightforward, something needs to be said about the textual variant around the word πιστεύ[σ]ητε in 20:31,[17] commonly translated "you may believe." The πιστεύητε reading, where the verb tense is present subjunctive, has been taken by scholars to suggest an edificatory purpose for the writing of the Gospel. In other words, John wrote in order to establish and confirm his readers in their faith in Jesus Christ. The other reading, πιστεύσητε (aorist subjunctive), has been taken to suggest an evangelistic purpose for the Gospel's writing. In other words, John wrote for a largely non-Christian readership in order to lead them to initial faith in Christ.

When we turn to the question of which reading has greater manuscript support, some scholars assumed that the evidence is finely balanced, suggesting that the question cannot be settled definitively.[18] But I concur with Gordon D. Fee's findings and conclusion that the present subjunctive has the support of notable early muscripts. Fee writes: "The primary Egyptians (P[66] ℵ B, the earliest and best MSS for this Gospel [P[75] is lacunose], plus some secondary witnesses from this tradition (0250 892) and the non-Egyptian Θ, form a considerable combination of evidence in favor of πιστεύητε."[19]

The next question is what significance we are to adduce, or what conclusion we are to derive, from John's use of the present subjunctive. Here one needs to be careful not to build a whole view of John's readership on the basis of the verb tense alone. That being said, it can be concluded that John's use of πιστεύητε supports (although it does not itself establish) the view that John's Gospel was written for a believing readership. This is the conclusion of several key interpreters (such as Fee[20]) who have analyzed the evidence.

Aside from the support provided by πιστεύητε in 20:31, the view that John wrote to a largely believing audience, the view espoused in this book,

---

17. Both the NA[28] and UBS[5] editions of the Greek NT indicate this expression.
18. E.g., Beasley-Murray, *John*, 387; Carson, "Purpose," 640.
19. Fee, "Text," 2195–96.
20. Fee, "Text," 2219–205.

can be established on other internal grounds. In the words of Andrew T. Lincoln:

> The witness of this book to the life, death and resurrection of Jesus is meant to produce continuance in belief. The shape of the argument, whereby implied readers are expected to share the point of view set out in the prologue if they are to appreciate the ironies of the unfolding story and then to be confirmed in this perspective by the time the narrative reaches its conclusion, also suggests that its primary purpose is to reinforce the faith of those who are already Christian believers. The account of Jesus' public mission is not formulated as if the intent were to make a case about Jesus to unbelievers. In particular, Jesus' discourses and disputes with opponents presuppose some knowledge on the part of the believing readers about the issues faced in their own time about Jesus' identity . . . In addition, implied readers are expected to identify in particular with the role of Jesus' followers in the narrative and a large portion of that narrative (chapters 13–17) is devoted to addressing explicitly the concerns of such followers. Quite different rhetorical strategies would be required if the aim were to persuade readers to come to initial belief.[21]

The precise life setting of this believing readership cannot be determined with absolute certainty. But the Gospel itself, particularly its threefold mention of ἀποσυνάγωγος, suggests that its Christian readers experienced some kind of persecution from surrounding Jewish circles (synagogue). For instance, in 9:22 the parents of the man blind from birth, whom Jesus has healed, are afraid of the "Jews" for they have already decided that anyone who confesses Jesus as the Messiah should be expelled from the synagogue. In 12:42 many, even of the authorities, did not make their faith in Jesus public because they were afraid to be ἀποσυνάγωγοι ("expelled from their synagogue"). In 16:2 the threat for being disciples of Jesus is not just expulsion from synagogues but also of being killed. From these passages and others we may glean that John wrote to believers (rather than unbelievers) who were needing not only encouragement to keep up their Christian faith but probably also a helpful presentation and defense of why Jesus is the true Messiah and Son of God. Probably the purpose was not simply to encourage them in the midst of hostility and persecution but also to equip them to respond appropriately to dissenting opinions about Jesus, with perhaps a more positive end-goal of sharing the faith.

21. Lincoln, *Gospel*, 87. See also Fee, "Text," 2204–5.

The Significance of the Johannine Temple Incident

John's purpose, its probable readership, the immediate religio-sociopolitical context in which it was written all shed light on our understanding of this Gospel—its themes, emphases, and distinctives. First, we note John's notable distinctives compared to the Synoptics. It leaves out the parables entirely, the transfiguration, the institution of the Lord's Supper, exorcisms, Jesus' temptation, and others. It includes many important details that the Synoptics leave out, such as the wine miracle in Cana, Jesus' conversation with Nicodemus, ministry in Samaria, the raising of Lazarus, Jesus' frequent journeys to Jerusalem, extended discourses in the temple, and others.

Second, John introduces Jesus to his readers as the Son of God, who preexisted with God the Father before he came into the world (1:1–18; 17:5). Keener writes, "Christology is John's central focus, as both the poem (1:1–18) and summary thesis statement (20:30–31) testify. Both of these passages emphasize the highest, most complete Johannine Christology: Jesus is deity (1:1, 18; 20:28–31)."[22] Third, other notable Johannine themes include eschatology, love, faith, life, and the world.[23]

John consists of a prologue (1:1–18), a body (1:19—20:31), and an epilogue (21:1–25). Below is an outline[24] of the Gospel, where our immediate passage is highlighted.

Main Division	First-Level Subdivision	Second-Level Subdivision	Third-Level Subdivision	Heading
1:1–18	Prologue			
1:19—20:31	The self-revelation of God through the incarnate Word			
		1:19—10:42	Jesus discloses himself in word and deed.	
			1:19–51	Prelude to Jesus' ministry
			1:19–28	John the Baptist in relation to Jesus
			1:29–34	The Baptist's witness to Jesus
			1:35–51	Jesus' first disciples
			2:1—4:54	Jesus' signs, works, and words
			2:1–11	Jesus turns water to wine

---

22. Keener, *Gospel*, 1:281.

23. Keener, *Gospel*, 320–30; see also Carson, *Gospel*, 95–100.

24. Adapted from Carson and Moo, *Introduction*, 225–29.

The Significance of the Temple Incident in the Narratives of the Four Gospels

		2:12–22	**Jesus clears the temple**
		2:23–25	The inadequate faith of many
		3:1–21	Jesus talks to Nicodemus
		3:22–36	The Baptist testifies about Jesus
		4:1–42	Jesus ministers in Samaria
		4:43–54	Jesus heals the royal official's son
	5:1—7:52	More signs, works, and words in the context of opposition	
		5:1–15	Jesus heals the paralytic
		5:16–30	Jesus' Sonship
		5:31–47	Testimonies about Jesus
		6:1–15	Jesus feeds the 5,000
		6:16–21	Jesus walks on water
		6:22–58	Discourse: Jesus the Bread of Life
		6:59–71	Many disciples desert Jesus
		7:1–13	Jesus attends the Feast of Tabernacles
		7:14–52	Jesus' confrontation with the Jewish authorities
	7:53—8:11	A woman caught in adultery	
	8:12—10:42	Climactic signs, words, and works in the context of radical transformation	
		8:12–59	Second round of confrontation with the Jewish authorities
		9:1–41	Jesus heals a man born blind
		10:1–21	Jesus the good Shepherd
		10:22–42	The unbelief of the "Jews"
11:1–12:50	Transition		

		11:1–44	The raising of Lazarus
		11:45–57	The plot to kill Jesus
		12:1–11	Jesus anointed at Bethany
		12:12–19	Jesus enters Jerusalem
		12:20–36	Jesus predicts his death
		12:37–50	The "Jews" persist in unbelief
	13:1—20:31	Jesus' self-disclosure through his death-and-resurrection	
		13:1–17	Jesus washes his disciples' feet
		13:18–30	Jesus predicts his betrayal
		13:31—16:33	Jesus' farewell discourse
		17:1–26	Jesus prays
		18:1—19:42	Jesus' trial and passion
		20:1–31	Jesus' resurrection
21:1–25	Epilogue		

The Narrative Contexts

In the following discussion I limit myself to two immediate narrative contexts of the Johannine temple incident: the wine miracle in Cana recounted in 2:1–11 and the statement of Jewish unbelief in 2:23–25.

The Wine Miracle at Cana (2:1–11)

The wine miracle in Cana (2:1–11) is significant for a number of reasons. First, it is an account not shared by the Synoptics. Second, in John's narrative design and structure, it is the first of the many recorded signs that Jesus performed (2:11; cf. 20:30–31). Third and most important for this book, this miracle serves as the immediate, preceding context of the temple incident.

John 2:1–4:54[25] is a whole section marked out with repeated references to Cana in 2:1 and in 4:46 forming an *inclusio*. This section is characterized

---

25. Refer to the above outline.

The Significance of the Temple Incident in the Narratives of the Four Gospels

by thematic unity: the theme is similar to the apostle Paul's message in 2 Cor 5:17, "The old has gone, the new has come!"[26] In Dodd's words,

> The three chapters present the replacement of the old purifications by the wine of the kingdom of God, the old temple by the new in the risen Lord, an exposition of new birth for new creation, a contrast between the water of Jacob's well and the living water from Christ, and the worship of Jerusalem and Gerizim with worship "in spirit and in truth."[27]

John's summary note in 2:11 is significant: "This—the first of Jesus' signs—he did at Cana in Galilee; he thereby manifested his glory, and his disciples believed in him." That John describes this miracle as the first of Jesus' signs indicates "its primacy among the wonders Christ wrought."[28] For R. F. Collins, this miracle is the key to the Johannine signs.[29] But in addition to the "firstness," this miracle is, more importantly, a "sign," a "symbol." Koester has reminded us that Johannine symbols or signs "can signify several things simultaneously."[30] What then is the significance of this miracle? As John calls it a sign, what it is a sign of?

Let us consider the implications of the evangelist's presenting this miracle as the first among Jesus' many signs. The implications are profound and will help us not only to locate the Johannine Jesus in his public ministry but also to understand his aims and why he speaks and acts the way he does. For example, we all ask the question why Jesus speaks in a seemingly impolite way to his mother. Also, and following from that, we grope for Jesus' meaning when he says that his "hour" has not yet come. What "hour"?

The emphasis on the "firstness" draws attention to the commencement of Jesus' public ministry. The God-appointed "hour" has not yet come for him to consummate his God-given mandate, he being the Messiah, the Christ, and the only hope of the whole world. In Edersheim's words,

> We behold Him now as freely mingling with humanity, sharing its joys and engagements, entering into its family life, sanctioning and hallowing all by His Presents and blessing; then as transforming

---

26. Carson, *Gospel*, 166.
27. Dodd, *Interpretation*, 297.
28. Toussaint, "Significance," 45.
29. Collins, *Studies*, 161.
30. Koester, *Symbolism*, 24. See pp. 76–77, for Koester's mechanics of how several interpretations of a sign can be shown to be correct while certain other interpretations can be shown to be false or wrong.

the "water of legal purification" into the wine of the new dispensation, and, more than this, the water of our felt want into the wine of His giving; and, lastly, as having absolute power as the "Son of Man," being also "the Son of God" and "King of Israel."[31]

The launch of Jesus' public ministry inevitably affects his life in two important ways, as we can see in 2:4, where Jesus says to his mother, "Woman, what concern is that to you and to me? My hour has not yet come." First, there is a huge implication to the way Jesus here addresses his mother which, as Haenchen correctly observes,[32] does not differ from the way he addresses the Samaritan woman (4:21) and Mary Magdalene (20:13). Our difficulty with Jesus' manner of speaking to his mother here owes to our understanding of Jesus' being a son—Mary's son. There is a flip side to that identity of course and Jesus' being Mary's son fades away in the face of Jesus' being God's Son now that Jesus has launched his public career. Carson has written aptly: "Now that he had entered into the purpose of his coming, everything, even family ties, had to be subordinated to his divine mission."[33] Haenchen also comments aptly:

> Jesus does not permit himself to be prompted to act by any human agent, even when that agent is his own mother; he is driven by the will of the Father alone. When Jesus then performs what is requested of him in a few minutes or a few days later, that is no contradiction in the eyes of the evangelist. It has nothing to do with a temporal interval, but with the fact that Jesus will only heed the divine call (7:13, 30).[34]

Second, Jesus' launching into his public ministry has huge implications on the state of things between him and Judaism. He signifies this in 2:4b, "My hour has not yet come." This statement, understood by itself, does not make sense as Jesus' reply to his mother's report, "They have no wine" (2:3b). It does not make sense if we take it to mean: "The hour for me to supply them

---

31. Edersheim, *Life*, 243–44.
32. Haenchen, *John*, 1:173.
33. Carson, *Gospel*, 171. See also Morris, *Gospel*, 180–81; Keener, *Gospel*, 505–06; Bultmann: "The miracle worker is bound to his own law and must listen to another voice" (quoted in Ashton, *Understanding*, 195); Brown (*Gospel*, 1:102): "Jesus is placing himself beyond natural family relationships even as he demanded of his disciples (Matthew xix:29)."
34. Haenchen, *John*, 1:173.

with wine"³⁵ has not yet come. What "hour," and how does it fit in the narrative? We must note here that ὥρα ("hour") is a word frequently occurring in the Fourth Gospel, and constantly it refers to Jesus' "death on the cross and the exaltation bound up with it (7:30; 8:20; 12:23, 27; 13:1; 17:1), or the consequences deriving from it (5:28–29)."³⁶ In Keener's words, "the 'hour' is the hour of the cross, the time of Jesus' impending death."³⁷

To those acquainted with John, the death of Jesus not just brings up the role of the Roman soldiers. More importantly it signifies the conflict between Jesus and Judaism. Jesus' message and actions were perceived by the Jewish establishment as a challenge and assault on their faith and traditions, and when they finally had enough, they had him nailed on the cross. Even right here in this miracle, as Jesus begins his public career, we see this confrontation playing out in the symbolism of the water and the pot, to which we shall return shortly. The question remains: "Why should the fact that it is not yet Jesus' time for passing to the Father in suffering and glory prohibit him from performing a miracle at the beginning of his ministry?" asks Ashton.³⁸ Notice the word "prohibit" in Ashton's question. Then he offers the answer that there was the risk of being misunderstood, to which Twelftree agrees.³⁹

However, Ashton's phrasing of the question appears problematic, for there are no indications in the text of Jesus' feeling or being prohibited from performing the miracle. Perhaps, Barclay's translation of 2:4 is more helpful: "Lady, let me handle this in my own way."⁴⁰ In sum, Jesus' statement of "my hour" must be understood as pointing to his death on the cross. Hence, his "hour" is not yet now. At the same time, because Jesus has launched his public ministry, we must understand his seeming impoliteness to Mary in light of his being the Messiah, the Son of God, not in light of his being Mary's son.

We turn now to an analysis of some key symbolisms in the miracle account that together with the above make this miracle programmatic and paradigmatic for the rest of the signs in the Fourth Gospel. We will also see how significantly related this miracle is to the subsequent account of

35. Barrett, *Gospel*, 159.
36. Carson, *Gospel*, 171.
37. Keener, *Gospel*, 1:507.
38. Ashton, *Understanding*, 195.
39. Twelftree, *Jesus*, 195.
40. Cited in Morris, *Gospel*, 18.

the temple incident. First, let us consider the symbolism of the wine being depleted, as reported in 2:3 ("the wine has run out"). If the Matthean and Markan fruitless fig tree which Jesus cursed represents a hollow and condemned Israel, can it also be that the failure of the wine supply at the Cana wedding feast represents a hollow Israel that stands under God's judgment? The Johannine answer to that seems to be a yes; it signifies disaster and God's judgment upon the failure of the Jewish religion.[41] This will be further corroborated as we move along.

Second, we inquire into the symbolism of the water jars in verse 6, which John describes as intended for Jewish ceremonial washing. Let us retrace the chain of events. In verse 3, the supply of wine runs out and Mary reports it to Jesus. In verse 4, Jesus answers his mother obliquely, seemingly not wanting to cooperate with her. In verse 5, Mary displays patience, submission, and faith by telling the servants (apparently, of the house) to do whatever Jesus says. Verse 6 tells us about six stone jars. Then we find Jesus in verse 7 instructing the servants to fill up the jars to the brim. Then the miracle happens: the water becomes wine! John's comment in verse 6 concerning the water jars ("the kind used by the Jews for ceremonial washing") unlocks the symbolism:

> They stand for the entire system of Jewish ceremonial observance—and by implication for religion upon that level, wherever it is found, as distinguished from religion upon the level of ἀλήθεια (cf. iv. 23–4). Thus the first of signs already symbolizes the doctrine that ὅτι ὁ νόμος διὰ Μωϋσέως ἐδόθη, ἡ χάρις καὶ ἡ ἀλήθεια διὰ Ἰησοῦ Χριστοῦ ἐγένετο.[42]

Carson supports this interpretation: "The water represents the old order of Jewish law and custom, which Jesus was to replace with something better."[43] Witherington is also of the same view: Jesus "is the one who brings the new wine of the Gospel, which eclipses and makes obsolete previous sources of life and health such as Jewish purification water." He continues: It presents "the faith that is centered on Jesus as a more powerful, life-giving, and universally accessible faith than Judaism."[44]

---

41. So Tweftree, *Jesus*, 192.
42. Dodd, *Interpretation*, 311.
43. Carson, *Gospel*, 173.
44. Witherington, *Wisdom*, 78.

Third, how about the symbolism of the wine itself, here in massive amounts?[45] What does it symbolize? Wine in the OT symbolizes physical and spiritual joy (Eccl 9:7; Gen 27:28), hope (Zech 10:6-7; Isa 25:6; Joel 2:19), and abundance (Joel 2:19; 3:18; Amos 9:13). Culpepper explains, "Jesus' coming as the fulfillment of Israel's hopes and eschatological expectations is therefore reflected in the provision of a bountiful amount of good wine."[46] In terms of a symbolic gesture, that is exactly what Jesus does here in Cana.

In sum, the miracle in Cana is clearly a programmatic sign in John. Not only does it mark the beginning of Jesus' public ministry; it also marks the beginning of Jesus' assault on the Jewish establishment. And in so far as that assault is concerned, this miracle therefore highlights the theme of confrontation that will play out again and again in the Gospel. In and through Jesus—his person, credentials, and achievements—God's kingdom has come and the Jewish religion is not only rendered powerless but also obsolete. Out of the water in the stone jars for Jewish ceremonial cleansing, Jesus has created a fresh, delicious, and superabundant wine, and this wine symbolizes God's blessings in and through Jesus. Jesus' statement, "My hour has not yet come," points proleptically to the culmination of that struggle with the Jewish authorities—his crucifixion. But his seeming defeat will turn into victory in his resurrection which is anticipated by John's comment in 2:1, "on the third day." This miracle, therefore, is the proper context for understanding the subsequent account of Jesus' protest in the Jerusalem temple to which we shall turn below.

The Inadequate Faith of the Jerusalemites (2:23-25)

As the wine miracle in Cana immediately precedes the Johannine temple incident, the account of the inadequate faith of the Jerusalemites in Jesus (2:23-25) immediately follows it. As commentators regularly point out, 2:23-25 is a transitional passage, linking the temple incident to the Nicodemus episode in John 3.

Three important points emerge from our passage. First, there is a summative reference to the signs of Jesus in verse 23. That is in spite of the fact

---

45. All the jars (pots) together could hold between 100 and 150 gallons (between 500 and 750 liters). The sheer quantity makes Haenchen conclude John here was exaggerating it (*John*, 1:173-74).

46. Culpepper, *Gospel*, 131.

that the evangelist has not actually recounted any specific sign, except for the temple incident.[47] The plurality of the signs that Jesus has performed in Jerusalem signifies his desire to reveal himself to the "Jews," particularly to those in Jerusalem. That includes the Jewish leaders—as referenced in the preceding account of the temple incident (to be discussed below)—as well as the common people of Jerusalem.

Second, there is a reference to the faith in Jesus of many Jerusalemites in verse 23. It is said that these Jerusalemites believed in Jesus because of the signs that he performed. This is, on the surface, a good outcome. It recalls the faith of the disciples in Jesus in 2:11 as a result of the wine miracle in Cana. It also appears to prospectively fulfill the evangelist's purpose for writing as enunciated in 20:30–31. However, it remains to be seen what sort of faith this is, for in John not every act of believing connotes true faith (more on this below).

Third, the evangelist tells us in verse 24 that Jesus rejects the faith of the Jerusalemites, and the reason is given in verse 25: "He did not need any man's testimony, for he knew what was in man." As Lincoln observes, "there is a type of belief which remains at the level of being impressed by the signs and fails to see through the signs to what they signify—the glory of Jesus in his oneness with God (see also 4.48; 7.3–5). This faith does not grasp the significance of Jesus' person and commit itself to the implications of that significance."[48] Hence, while the belief of the Jerusalemites recalls the belief of the disciples in 2:11, their faiths are qualitatively different. The faith of the disciples is genuine, while that of the Jerusalemites falls short of genuine Johannine faith, bordering only at the level of admiration.[49]

In sum, it appears that Jesus' first ministry-journey to the capital of the nation and the heart of Judaism yields no significant result in terms of people coming to true faith in him. That is in spite of his significant self-revelatory deeds. The Jewish leaders reject him (to be discussed below) and ordinary Jerusalemites admire his deeds but fail to discern his true identity. We turn now to the temple incident itself.

---

47. In *The Cross-and-Resurrection* (forthcoming), I argue in favor of construing the temple incident as a σημεῖον. See also Vistar, "Supreme Σημεῖον"; Lincoln, *Gospel*, 145.

48. Lincoln, *Gospel*, 145..

49. See Vistar, "Σημεῖον."

The Significance of the Temple Incident in the Narratives of the Four Gospels

ANALYSIS OF THE TEMPLE INCIDENT PERICOPE (VV. 13-22)

John recounts the temple incident as follows:

> 13 The Passover of the Jews was near, and Jesus went up to Jerusalem. 14 In the temple he found people selling cattle, sheep, and doves, and the money-changers seated at their tables. 15 Making a whip of cords, he drove all of them out of the temple, both the sheep and the cattle. He also poured out the coins of the money-changers and overturned their tables. 16 He told those who were selling the doves, "Take these things out of here! Stop making my Father's house a marketplace!" 17 His disciples remembered that it was written, "Zeal for your house will consume me." 18 The Jews then said to him, "What sign can you show us for doing this?" 19 Jesus answered them, "Destroy this temple, and in three days I will raise it up." 20 The Jews then said, "This temple has been under construction for forty-six years, and will you raise it up in three days?" 21 But he was speaking of the temple of his body. 22 After he was raised from the dead, his disciples remembered that he had said this; and they believed the scripture and the word which Jesus had spoken.

Introductory Comments

A cursory look at the Fourth Gospel's outline above and at Appendix 1 readily reveals three basic differences between the Johannine account of the temple incident and that of the Synoptic Gospels. First, in terms of placement and chronology, John situates the temple incident in the beginning of Jesus' public ministry, whereas the Synoptics situate it at the end, at the onset of Jesus' passion week. Second, John's immediate context of the temple incident is the miracle in Cana, whereas in the Synoptics it is Jesus' entry into Jerusalem (plus, the fig tree incident in Matthew and Mark). Third, in terms of specific details, John's account differs in a number of ways from that of the Synoptics (to be discussed below).

How to account for all these differences is by no means an easy task. As Borchert observes, "Perhaps no other text in the Gospel of John has created greater problems for historians than the positioning of the cleansing of the temple at this point in John."[50] Scholars have long debated which

---

50. Borchert, *John 1-11*, 160.

The Significance of the Johannine Temple Incident

chronology is more reflective of history. The vast majority of scholars (for example: Dodd, Lightfoot, and Barrett)[51] argue for the priority of the Synoptic chronology, while a few others (notably Robinson)[52] argue for the priority of the Johannine chronology. A few others refuse to pit the Synoptic and Johannine chronologies by postulating two "cleansings," one that happened at the beginning of Jesus' public ministry (reported by John) and another during the last week of Jesus' earthly life and ministry (reported by the Synoptics).[53]

The position taken in this book is that there was probably only one "cleansing," which, based on the Synoptic chronology, took place during the final week of Jesus' life and public ministry. My reasons are as follows. First, none of the four Gospels provide any indication that the temple incident happened twice. If indeed Jesus "cleansed" the temple twice, first at the beginning of his ministry and another at the end, one wonders why not even one of the evangelists preserves any knowledge of this. In fact, it would probably have served the purposes of the evangelists (for instance, in the case of Mark, his purpose of showing how the temple cleansing was definitive to Jesus' crucifixion; in the case of John, his purpose of showing Jesus' assault on Jewish establishments) to make reference to two cleansings if indeed it happened twice. Since none of the four Gospels provide any evidence of a twofold temple "cleansing," this hypothesis cannot be taken seriously.

Second, from the accounts of the four evangelists of the temple incident, we get a clear sense that the incident is pretty serious in that the Jewish authorities uniformly respond to Jesus' provocative actions with a threat to his life. This is especially so in the Synoptic accounts, where the temple incident serves as the precipitating cause for Jesus' arrest, trials, and death. But this is also true of the Johannine version of the incident, where the enigmatic talk of the destruction and raising up of the "temple" actually pertains to Jesus' death-and-resurrection (to be discussed below). In light of this, the twofold temple "cleansing" hypothesis does not seem to be reasonable, for, based on evidence, it is not likely that the temple authorities would allow Jesus to perform a provocative act twice.

---

51. Dodd, *Interpretation*, 297–300; Lightfoot, "Cleansing"; Lightfoot, *Gospel*, 60–79; Barrett, *Gospel*, 162–64.

52. Robinson, *Priority*, passim.

53. Hendricksen, *Exposition*, 1:120; Carson, *Gospel*, 177–78; Morris, *Gospel*, 166–69; Chapple, "Intervention."

Finally, as scholars have already pointed out,[54] and as we will soon show below, John's account of the incident resembles those of the Synoptics in terms of the key outline, and Brown has noted three features of correspondence: Jesus' action/protest (John 2:14–16 // Mark 11:15–18); the Jews' questioning of Jesus' authority (John 2:18 // Mark 11:28); and the prophecy of the destruction of the temple (John 2:19 // Mark 14:58; 15:29).[55] Therefore, it is more likely that there was only one cleansing, and that John appears to have transposed the "cleansing" toward the beginning of Jesus' career for his own theological purposes.[56]

Structure

The Johannine temple incident, though intricately connected to the previous account of the wedding in Cana, is a self-contained pericope that has a clear beginning, body, and conclusion, though its conclusion is open-ended "pointing forward to the conclusion of the drama in the death and resurrection of Jesus."[57] It may be helpful to look at three different outlines of the passage by various scholars. Joachim Gnilka outlines the passage as follows:[58]

1. Jesus' protest (2:13–16)

2. The disciples' remembrance (2:17)

3. Jesus' dispute with the "Jews" (2:18–21)

4. The disciples' remembrance (2:22)

This outline clearly shows that Jesus' protest results in his dispute with the "Jews," as well as the twofold references to the disciples' remembrance. Another outline worth looking at is that of Rudolf Schnackenburg, who arranges the passage as a diptych.[59]

---

54. Haenchen, *John*, 196; Witherington, *Wisdom*, 85–86.

55. Cited in Lindars, *Gospel*, 136.

56. See Michaels, *John*, 50; Borchert, *John*, 160–61; Keener, *Gospel*, 1:517–22; Lindars, *Gospel*, 135–37; France, "Chronological Aspects," 41–42; Whitacre, *John*, 82; Painter, *Quest*, 192; Dodd, *Interpretation*, 300–303; Witherington, *Wisdom*, 85–86.

57. Witherington, *Wisdom*, 85.

58. Cited in Chanikuzhy, *Jesus*, 240.

59. Schnackenburg, *Gospel*, 1:344. This outline resembles that of Beasley-Murray (*John*, 38) and Witherington (*Wisdom*, 85).

A. 1. Jesus' action (2:14–15)

   2. Jesus' words (2:16)

   3. The disciples' remembering (2:17)

B. 1. The Jews' action (2:18)

   2. Jesus' words (2:19)

   3. The Jews' misunderstanding (2:20–21)

   4. The disciples' remembering (2:22)

Finally, here is Mary Coloe's outline of the passage:[60]

1. Introduction (2:13)

2. Temple action (2:14–17)

3. Temple logion (2:18–22)

4. Conclusion (2:23–25)

Though these outlines are not identical, they nevertheless highlight the same key features of the text: (1) Jesus starts the action in the temple precinct; he issues his protest against the mercantile activities happening there; (2) without delay, Jesus protest is met with opposition from the "Jews," challenging his authority; and (3) on two counts (vv. 17, 22), John calls our attention to the disciples' "remembering," showing their maturing understanding of the meaning and significance of Jesus' action.

The Setting of the Incident

Verse 13 tells us the temporal setting of the incident: the Jewish Passover was "at hand." Despite the chronological differences noted above, this festal context is affirmed by the Synoptics (following Jesus' entry to Jerusalem which marked the beginning of Jesus' passion week, also on Passover feast).[61] Verse 13 goes on to tell us that Jesus "went up to Jerusalem." During the time of Jesus, Passover was one of the pilgrimage festivals where Jews from Judea, Galilee, and the Diaspora travelled to Jerusalem to participate in festal observances in the temple.[62] But, as the ensuing actions in

---

60. Coloe, *God Dwells*, 70–71.
61. See, e.g., Matt 26:17–18; Mark 14:1–2, 12–15; Luke 22:7–8.
62. See my discussion of this in "Σημεῖον," 117–19.

the temple courts will soon reveal (to be discussed below), Jesus does not undertake this pilgrimage as would a normal, ordinary devout Jew. He goes to Jerusalem and to the temple as the incarnate λόγος ("Word") of the Father (1:1-2, 14), as the Father's ultimate revealer (1:18), as ὁ ἀμνὸς τοῦ θεοῦ ("the Lamb of God") (1:29, 36), as the one of whom Moses and the prophets wrote (1:45), as ὁ υἱὸς τοῦ θεοῦ ("the Son of God") (1:49), as ὁ βασιλεὺς τοῦ Ἰσραήλ ("the King of Israel") (1:45), and as ὁ υἱὸς τοῦ ἀνθρώπου ("the Son of Man") (1:51).

The location of Jesus' protest is described as ἐν τῷ ἱερῷ ("in the temple"). We have already established in the previous chapters that in the first instance, ἱερόν ("temple"), when used of the Jerusalem temple, refers to the temple complex as a whole, including the various courts as well as the covered porticos. It is to be distinguished from ναός, which pertains narrowly to the sanctuary. But here in 2:14, as commentators regularly point out, ἱερόν more narrowly and specifically pertains to what has come to be known as the Court of the Gentiles, so called because Gentile converts to Judaism were permitted to enter there and participate in the worship of Yahweh. These references to Passover and the temple set this story in the context of Jewish cultic worship.[63]

The narrative proceeds by describing what is inside the temple precincts, in verse 14, to pave the way for Jesus' protest in verse 15: "In the temple he found people selling cattle, sheep, and doves, and the money-changers seated at their tables." We have here the basic elements of the Jewish cultic worship: the animal offerings for the sacrificial system and the temple tax. The sale of animals in the Court of the Gentiles owes to the fact that not all worshipers are able to bring their sacrificial animals, which have to be up to the approved standards, to the temple. This is especially so for pilgrim-worshipers coming from Galilee and farther afield in the Diaspora. So the availability of animals in the temple premises is a convenience for many people.

The same observation can be said of the currency exchange services. Jewish males, twenty years old and over, are mandated by the Torah to pay the annual half-shekel temple tax.[64] This needs to be paid in the acceptable currency, which was in Tyrian coinage.[65] Worshipers from outside Palestine

---

63. So Coloe, *God Dwells*, 71.

64. See Exod 30:11-16; Neh 10:32; Matt 17:24-27; Josephus, *B.J.* 7.218; *A.J.* 3.194-96; Philo, *Spec. Laws* 1.78.

65. *t. Ketub.* 13:3; *m. Bek.* 8:7.

The Significance of the Johannine Temple Incident

carrying different coins need help to have those coins exchanged for the acceptable ones. Thus there are moneychangers in the temple courtyards, sitting at their tables, offering services for a fee.

One can easily discern John's emphasis in verse 14 on Jesus' encounter with the Jewish cult. It is worth noting that while Matthew and Luke generally refer to buying and selling in the temple courts and Mark only mentions the money-exchange services and the selling of doves, John adds the reference to the selling of cattle and sheep. So there appears to be a heightened stress in John on the Jewish sacrificial worship, all in the context of the temple and the Passover feast. All this creates a rich web of Christological meaning when construed in light of Jesus' identity spelled out in John 1, particularly John's firm claim that Jesus is the supreme revelation of the Father (vv. 1–2, 18), that Jesus is the true tabernacle and temple (v. 14) and that he is the lamb of God that takes away the sin (not just of Israel but) of the whole world (vv. 29, 36).

Jesus' Prophetic Actions (vv. 15–16)

What Jesus does upon seeing the sacrificial animals and the money-exchange services in the temple courts heightens the dramatic and symbolic nature of the scene.

Jesus is so much displeased, to the point of being enraged, by the mercantile activities going on in the temple precincts (v. 14), so that he without delay takes action. John records Jesus' response in verses 15–16.

> So he made a whip of cords, and drove all from the temple courts, both sheep and cattle; he scattered the coins of the money-changers and overturned their tables. To those who sold doves he said, "Get these out of here! Stop turning my Father's house into a market!"

That Jesus makes a whip is unique to John. The Synoptics do tell us of Jesus' driving out the sellers and buyers from the temple, but they do not refer to a whip. We may assume that Jesus did not carry this whip from outside into the temple precincts, for "weapons were forbidden in the temple area. The Mishnah forbids one to bring a staff (*maqqēl*) into the temple (*m. Ber.* 9:5)."[66] What kind of whip did Jesus use? John uses the word φραγέλλιον,[67]

---

66. Croy, "Whippersnapper," 556.

67. There are two textual variants surrounding this term. Some manuscripts (namely ℵ A B Δ Θ Ψ and so forth) have φραγέλλιον only, whereas other manuscripts (namely P[66]

which can refer to a whip "consisting of a thong or thongs, frequently with metal tips to increase the severity of the punishment."[68] This noun occurs only here in the NT and nowhere in the LXX. Two things in the text will be helpful for our understanding. First, John implies that Jesus made this whip on the spot. Second, John says that the whip was made ἐκ σχοινίων ("from cords"). These cords would have been the materials available on the grounds of the temple precincts, and Neufeld suggests that it might have been "a straw lying about"[69] while Croy thinks that "this material might have been available as the animals' bedding or perhaps was already fashioned into ropes or traces."[70] It seems clear that Jesus makes this whip on the spot using whatever material he could find on the grounds of the temple precincts. There are no indications in the text that Jesus attached metals to this whip.

The next question arising from John 2:15 is, are we to understand Jesus as using the whip to drive out *only* the animals or *both* the animals *and* their sellers? Many scholars argue based on the gender of πάντας (masculine) that Jesus drove *all*—the sellers and their animals—out of the temple. R. E. Brown takes πάντας to refer to the sellers and their animals taken together as a unit; notice his translation of John 2:14–15, "In the temple precincts he came upon people engaged in selling oxen, sheep, and doves, and others seated, changing coins. So he made a [kind of] whip out of cords and drove the whole pack of them out of the temple area with their sheep and oxen."[71] H. K. Moulton argues that technically speaking πάντας should be referring to all the masculine object-nouns in the passage, such the sellers and the cattle, but not the sheep (neuter).[72] C. K. Barrett argues like Moulton: "πάντας (masculine) indicates that Jesus drove out all the *men* engaged in

---

P[75] G L N W[supp] and so forth) add ὡς before φραγέλλιον. The difference is, according to the first attestation, Jesus "made a whip," whereas according to the second, Jesus "made something like a whip." The New Testament Greek (UBS) follows the first attestation (see Metzger, *Commentary*, 173). Some contemporary scholars argue for the second attestation (Croy, "Whippersnapper," 557; Haenchen, *John*, 1:183). The first attestation is more likely to be original and ὡς to be a later scribal addition because it is more likely for the scribes to add this word in order to lessen the seemingly violent import of Jesus action. If ὡς had been in the original text, scribes would not have omitted it because doing so would heighten the violence of Jesus' action.

68. BAGD, s.v. "φραγέλλιον," 1064.
69. Neufeld, *Killing Enmity*,, 61.
70. Croy, "Whippersnapper," 557.
71. Brown, *Gospel*, 1:114.
72. Moulton, "*Pantas*," 127.

trade; if τά τε . . . βόας . . . had been intended as a merely epexegetical phrase we should have had πάντα, not πάντας."⁷³

Other interpreters⁷⁴ have difficulty with the interpretation that Jesus used the whip to drive out the sellers and their animals. Admittedly, that Jesus would use a whip on people does not cohere with the Gospels' portrait of Jesus as a man of peace. That is why certain scholars limit the referent of πάντας (masculine) to the animals (τά τε πρόβατα καὶ τοὺς βόας, neuter), even though πάντας is not compatible with τά πρόβατα. Keener passes over this grammatical difficulty and bases his conclusion on the passage's logic: "That Jesus must address the sellers, who are still present in 2:16, suggests that he has not struck them with the whip."⁷⁵ Dodd addresses the grammatical issue, "Here the τε . . . καὶ clause should in accord with normal usage, be epexegetical of πάντας . . . The masculine can be used where nouns of different genders are comprehended in a collective term. Thus the meaning would be 'he drove them all out, viz. sheep and oxen alike.'"⁷⁶ Dodd's conclusion agrees with the way the NRSV translates John 2:14–15, "In the temple, he found people selling cattle, sheep, and doves, and the money-changers seated at their tables. Making a whip of cords, he drove all of them out of the temple, both the sheep and the cattle." Notice that the phrase "both the sheep and the cattle" limits the referent of "all" (πάντας), thereby excluding the sellers.

In addition to Dodd's point, there are other supports for concluding that πάντας refers only to the sheep and cattle. First, John's reference to Jesus' making a whip is necessitated and explained by his reference to cattle and sheep. We recall that the Synoptics do not refer to cattle and sheep and hence they also do not refer to Jesus' making a whip. All this implies that Jesus makes the whip for a use on the animals, not on people. Second, it is correct that Jesus' whipping on the sellers in the temple would be deeply incompatible with Jesus' nature, calling, and motivations. Sure, exegesis informs our Christology, but this relationship is not a one-way traffic. Our systematic theology equally informs our exegesis. Jennifer Glancy's argument that Jesus indeed used violence though for symbolic purposes

---

73. Barrett, *Gospel*, 197.

74. Besides Keener and Dodd, see also Haenchen, *John*, 1:183; Hoskyns, *Gospel*, 194; Croy, "Whippersnapper," 559–63; Matson, "Contribution," 499 n. 55.

75. Keener, *Gospel*, 1:522.

76. Dodd, *Interpretation*, 156 n. 3.

is not justified textually, logically, and theologically.⁷⁷ That Jesus allowed violence to be done to his body on the cross does not necessitate Jesus' actually whipping people violently in the temple in order to convey a symbolic meaning. I find Glancy's study to be flawed. Her argument is that indeed Jesus whipped his fellow Jews on the temple and he did so as a form of symbolic communication. I have a problem with the suggestion that for Jesus to successfully send his message to the Jewish leaders in the temple, he had to inflict physical harm on the sellers there. Why would Jesus do that? Even in Mark's Gospel, where Jesus' protest in the temple is presented as directly the cause of his crucifixion, there is no reference to Jesus' whipping the sellers. Yes it is true that John was anxious to portray Jesus in opposition to the Jewish establishment, but there is nothing in John's text that supports Glancy's conclusions.

John 2:16 is largely unparalleled, καὶ τοῖς τὰς περιστερὰς πωλοῦσιν εἶπεν, ἄρατε ταῦτα ἐντεῦθεν, μὴ ποιεῖτε τὸν οἶκον τοῦ πατρός μου οἶκον ἐμπορίου. John presents Jesus as speaking to the sellers of doves, saying: "Get these out of here!" Jesus could not drive the doves out using the whip as he did with the cattle and sheep. It is likely that the doves were in metal or wooden cages and Jesus would therefore need the cooperation of the dove-sellers if the temple precincts were to be cleared of these birds. Then he said: μὴ ποιεῖτε τὸν οἶκον τοῦ πατρός μου οἶκον ἐμπορίου ("Stop making my Father's house a house of trade").⁷⁸ Jesus' point is quite clear and Carson explains it well: "Instead of solemn dignity and the murmur of prayer, there is the bellowing of cattle and the bleating of sheep. Instead of brokenness and contrition, holy adoration and prolonged petition, there is noisy commerce."⁷⁹

Scholars have rightly seen allusions in this text to OT prophetic passages such as Zech 14:21, "And on that day there will be no longer a merchant in the house of the Lord Almighty,"⁸⁰ and to Mal 3:1, 3, "Then suddenly the Lord you are seeking will come to his temple . . . he will purify the Levites and refine them like gold and silver." When Jesus calls the temple "his Father's house," he is of course pressing certain claims. First,

77. Glancy, "Violence," passim.

78. The grammatical construction μή plus ποιεῖτε (pres. imper.) has the effect of stopping something that is already happening or in existence (see BDF §336).

79. Carson, *Gospel*, 179.

80. See Chanikuzhy, *Jesus*, 258–64 for extended discussion and relevant secondary literature.

the Father here is Yahweh himself, Israel's covenant God, and Jesus calls him his Father. Second, notice that Jesus calls the temple his Father's house. Combine these two claims, and what is the conclusion? The temple is also Jesus' house because it belongs to his Father.[81] Nereparampil explains this Father-Son relationship this way:

> Everything that the Father has is the Son's and everything that the Son has is the Father's (Jn 17.10; 16.15). Jesus, therefore, appears in the Temple as the Son in the house. He conducts himself as the LORD of the Temple. By the Temple cleansing therefore, Jesus was manifesting himself as the Son of God who came to defend the honor of his Father.[82]

This truth then is the legitimization and warrant for Jesus' driving out the animals and the sellers from the temple. If anyone would ask him why he was doing all this, he could just easily say, "This temple, this house, is my property, and you are guilty of misusing it, abusing it, and you are bound to my Father's judgment." Of course, the Jews did not understand all this at the time of its occurrence.

We are to understand John's comment in 2:17 as meaning that right in the occurrence of Jesus' protest in the temple, the disciples that were with him interpreted his actions in the light of Ps 69:9 LXX, "Zeal for thy house will consume me," except that the verb tense has been changed from past to future.[83] Of course the disciples' association of Jesus' action to an OT passage has its background in their rootedness in the Jewish Scriptures and in the Jewish tradition of zeal for God's law and temple, and historically at times this zeal had taken on violent expressions. This observation does not, however, decide in favor of Jesus' whipping the sellers in verse 16. Supposing that Jesus had no whip in hand, his driving out the sellers, the animals, overturning tables, and rebuking people was in itself a spectacular display of zeal for the house of his Father.

---

81. See Moloney, *Gospel*, 441–42.

82. Nereparampil, *Temple*, 14.

83. Witherington (*Wisdon*, 88) suggests that this verbal change alludes to Jesus' death, especially because his death "seems in part to have been precipitated by [his] zeal for and action in his Father's house."

The Significance of the Temple Incident in the Narratives of the Four Gospels

Jesus' Confrontation with the "Jews" (2:18–22)[84]

Jesus' provocative protest in the temple courts brought him into direct confrontation with the "Jews." Οἱ Ἰουδαῖοι ("the Jews") of verse 18 should be understood as the Jewish leaders—either the temple authorities or representatives from the Sanhedrin.[85] They demanded Jesus to provide a σημεῖον ("sign") as justification for his actions,[86] whereas in Mark they questioned his authority.

What is a σημεῖον? Although it has been translated as "miracle" or "sign," σημεῖον has deeper and symbolic function or character.[87] Kerr notes three important things about σημεῖον in John. First, Jesus is its "exclusive" doer or author (10:41; 5:17). Second, the true understanding of a σημεῖον is reserved for the believer (6:26; 12:37). Third, its purpose is to show who Jesus is and lead people into genuine (Johannine) faith in him (4:48; 2:11, 23; 6:30; 12:37) as the Son of God and Messiah for their salvation (1:12; 3:16, 18; 20:30–31).[88] In John 2:18, the specific kind of σημεῖον requested is "a miraculous proof to guarantee belief."[89]

Jesus' response to the Jewish leaders, in verse 19, is rather unexpected and proves to be puzzling to the Jewish leaders (and even to his own disciples, v. 22). He speaks to them saying, λύσατε τὸν ναὸν τοῦτον καὶ ἐν τρισὶν ἡμέραις ἐγερῶ αὐτόν ("Destroy this temple and I will raise it again in three days"). This is a wise answer from Jesus in the sense that he involves the Jewish leaders in it: "Destroy this temple." In the first place, what Jesus is proposing is outrageous and unprecedented: the Jewish leaders would never conceive of destroying the temple! Even the thought of it is a blasphemous and a horrible thing. Secondly, it would require an army of heavy machines to destroy this temple, as the Jewish leaders themselves imply in verse 19. And yet Jesus is enigmatically enjoining them, in response to their very request, to destroy this temple, and that he would restore it "in

---

84. Refer to Appendix 3 for a comparison of John's and Mark's accounts of the incident.

85. Carson, *Gospel*, 180.

86. Carson (*Gospel*, 181) suggests that the Jewish leaders' demanding a sign "demonstrates [that] they harbored at least a suspicion that they were dealing with a heaven-sent prophet."

87. Σημεῖον basically refers to something by which a thing is known (LSJ, s.v. "σημεῖον," 1593; BDAG, s.v. "σημεῖον," 920; GELS, s.v. "σημεῖον," 620; Kerr, *Temple*, 86).

88. See related discussion in Chanikuzhy, *Jesus*, 291–96.

89. Moloney, *Gospel*, 444 n. 42; see also Witherington, *Wisdom*, 88.

three days" (we shall return to this phrase below). Carson thinks that Jesus' proposal, if carried out, would have been "a marvelously appropriate sign: anyone who could restore the temple within three days of its complete destruction must be judged to have the authority to regulate its practices."[90]

Verse 20 indicates that the "Jews" misunderstand Jesus' utterance; they take Jesus' statement quite literally to refer to the physical temple. We recall that in the Synoptic accounts of Jesus' trial before the Sanhedrin, he is charged with issuing a similar threat against the temple. He is accused of having said: "I will destroy this man-made temple and in three days will build another, not made by man" (Mark 14:58 pars.; cf. Mark 15:29). This is not exactly what Jesus said in John 2:19, but two elements connect the two accounts: the reference to the destruction and rebuilding of the temple and the concept of "after three days." Comparing what the false witnesses allege as Jesus' threat towards the temple to what Jesus said as John has recorded it, we realize that Jesus has been faulted twice: his immediate hearers in the temple misunderstand his meaning and then, in a matter of a few days (based on the assumption that there was only one cleansing of the temple and that it took place in the beginning of Jesus' passion week), during that court hearing before the Sanhedrin, the false witnesses misquote him. First, Jesus actually says "[*You*] destroy this temple," not "*I* will destroy this temple." Second, Jesus just says "temple," not "man-made temple . . . build another, not made by man" as the false witnesses allege.

We see in verse 22 that even Jesus' disciples, John himself included, do not immediately understand Jesus' statement back in verse 19. It is likely that they also take Jesus' mention of ναός to be referring to the physical temple. An explanation of this term is in order. It is a word that occurs in John only in this pericope (2:19, 20, 21). According to BAGD, ναός can have the following meanings: (1) temple in general (Acts 2:17); (2) the shrine where a deity's image was set up (3 Macc 1:10); (3) the Jerusalem temple (Matt 23:17, 35; 27:5, 40; Mark 14:58; Luke 1:21; Acts 7:48); (4) the heavenly sanctuary (Rev 14:15; 5:6, 8; 16:1, 17); (5) as an imagery for the human body (1 Cor 6:19); (6) as an imagery for the church (1 Cor 3:16, 17; 2 Cor 6:16; Eph 2:21).[91] As Chanikuzhy has pointed out, Jesus has referred to the physical temple in 2:14–15 by the term ἱερόν.[92] Then in 2:16, he calls that same ἱερόν as ὁ οἶκος τοῦ πατρός μου ("the house of my Father"). Now

---

90. Carson, *Gospel*, 181.
91. BDAG, s.v. "ναός," 665–66.
92. Chanikuzhy, *Jesus*, 306.

in 2:19, he uses ναός. Despite the shifts of words, the Jewish leaders' reaction in 2:20 indicates that they understand ναός to be referring to the whole temple structure, not only the sanctuary proper. Of course, we know on the basis of John's comment in 2:21 that they totally misunderstand Jesus. According to John, Jesus is in fact talking about his own body, not the Jerusalem temple.[93] That being the case, we come to a number of realizations. First, we realize that Jesus actually did not deny the demand of the Jewish leaders for a sign (2:18). He would give them that sign—his very death and resurrection.[94]

Second, by saying "Destroy this temple" (v. 19a), Jesus is actually prophetically saying that he would die (be destroyed) because of the Jewish leaders' prime responsibility. Third, we come to a very profound realization of Jesus' body as the true temple, recalling the notion of the incarnation of God's eternal λόγος in the Prologue. Carson is worth quoting at length.

> The Father and the *incarnate* Son enjoy unique mutual indwelling (14:10–11). Therefore it is the human body of Jesus that uniquely manifests the Father, and becomes the focal point of the manifestation of God to man, the living abode of God on earth, the fulfillment of all [that] the temple meant, and the center of all true worship (over against all other claims of "holy space," 4:20–24). In this "temple" the ultimate sacrifice would take place; within three days of death and burial, Jesus Christ, the true temple, would rise from the dead.[95]

SUMMARY AND CONCLUSION

Our study of the Johannine temple incident and its surrounding contexts has significantly manifested the way Jesus looked at the Judaism of his day according to John's unique presentation. We have seen many textual and literary indications of John's ability and prowess both as a historian and a

---

93. Nereparampil (*Temple*, 45–49) has argued, based on his understanding of the LXX's usages of ἱερόν and ναός, that John "always refers to the Jerusalem temple by *hieron*, never *naos*, except for the enigmatic saying of 2:19.. . . The real temple (*naos*) is now the *soma* of Jesus (2:21). Jesus is the true *naos*." See also Kerr, *Temple*, 88–89.

94. This is, in brief, my central argument in *The Cross-and-Resurrection* (forthcoming).

95. Carson, *Gospel*, 182. Carson warns, correctly, against interpreting the ναός of John 2:19 as meaning the church (in terms of the apostle Paul as in Rom 12:5 and 1 Cor 12:12ff.), "for *that* body was not first destroyed before it is raised up."

theologian. He recorded history for us, and this account is fashioned by his understanding of who Jesus is and how Jesus is supposed to be situated in relation to the Jewish religion.

The main point of the temple incident in John is that Jesus' body is the new temple (2:21). That statement is in itself a summary of the Christian gospel. Let us look at this from two angles. First, in and through Jesus' body, which was destroyed and raised again on the third day, God's intents, purposes, and aspirations symbolized by the Jewish temple were all fulfilled and accomplished. The Jewish temple was a shadow of the reality which is Jesus. The Jewish temple was the promise which found fulfillment in Jesus. This being the case, Jesus has replaced the temple. Jesus *is* the temple, the *new* temple. The Jewish temple no longer possesses the symbolic, typological import that it once possessed. In that sense, it is now obsolete.

In addition to the usual details, John's unique reference to cattle and sheep in the temple precincts and to Jesus' using a whip to drive these animals out of the temple strongly conveys not only God's judgment on the temple, not only Jesus' protest at the unacceptable mercantile practices going on in the temple, but also, and perhaps most importantly, the truth that the new temple, Jesus, has come. This truth has contextual support in Jesus' action in the wedding feast at Cana where, out of the water from the jars meant for Jewish ceremonial washing, Jesus has made abundant wine for the wedding feast.

Secondly, Jesus' body as the temple would undergo what he has hinted at in his reply to the Jewish leaders' demand: "Destroy this temple and I will raise it again on the third day" (2:19). By saying that, Jesus prophesied that he would die at the instigation of the Jewish leaders. John is anxious to clearly show us the conflict between Jesus and Judaism. Whereas the Synoptics, by placing the temple incident at the beginning of Jesus' passion week, foreground the intense struggle between Jesus and the Jewish leaders in a one-week period, John, by placing the temple incident at the beginning of Jesus' public ministry, foregrounds that same intense and fateful struggle in a three-year period (on the assumption that Jesus' public ministry lasted for three years). Hence, the meaning of Jesus' temple act becomes paradigmatic and programmatic in our hermeneutics of John 2 onwards. That means that John wants us to view the whole three-year public ministry of Jesus as not only generating conflicts with the Jewish leadership but also as consisting of those conflicts and in fact Jesus' death would be the culmination of those same conflicts.

The Significance of the Temple Incident in the Narratives of the Four Gospels

This chapter ends with a quote from Joel R. Wohlgemut, a quote that connects Jesus' body as temple to the church as also temple:

> Where does God dwell? According to the community looking through the Fourth Gospel, God is found—contrary to most expectations—not in the Jerusalem temple (or, by extension, Judaism), but in Jesus. However, the self-giving death and subsequent resurrection of this Jesus create the possibility of God's residence within the Christian community itself; the followers of Christ are the "temple" of God. This means that today's believing community is the "place" where God dwells.[96]

---

96. Wohlgemut, "Where Does God Dwell," 92.

6

Synthesis and Conclusions

OUR UNDERSTANDING OF JESUS' protest in the temple is bound to be richer, fuller, and deeper, thanks to the evangelists' inclusion of this incident in their respective Gospel accounts. The four accounts of the one incident are comparable to a diamond. We are looking at one diamond that is multi-faceted, rich, complex, and colorfully beautiful. The evangelists drew on a historical happening in the life of Christ and each of them crafted his report in accordance to his authorial, literary, and theological purposes. Hence, the differences in emphases, perspectives, and, on a few counts, in details. These differences, however, do not necessarily suggest contradictions.[1]

The question that this book has sought to answer has been: What is the significance of Jesus' temple act in the narrative design of each of the canonical Gospels? I have used a variation of composition criticism as my methodology, which focuses on the Gospel text itself, on the Gospel's historical backgrounds, and on the evangelist's theology. Using this methodology I have analyzed the temple incident in each of the four Gospels. The summary and synthesis of my findings are indicated in the following table.

---

1. See, for example, Licona, *Differences*, passim.

	Matt 21:12–13	Mark 11:15–19	Luke 19:45–46	John 2:13–22
Key themes and/or emphases	1. It is as the prophesied Davidic Messiah, with succinct emphasis on his authority, that Jesus enters the temple and issues his actions there. 2. Attention is paid to the distinct contrast between God's intention for the temple (to be "a house of prayer") and what the "Jews" made the temple to be ("a den of robbers"). An emphasis on the culpability of the "Jews" should be seen here as well. 3. It is in reaction to the "Jewish" desecration of the temple that Jesus issues his protest. 4. Jesus is concerned about the temple becoming "a house of prayer." Right after his protest, in the temple children acclaim him as the Son of David, and he proceeds to heal the blind and the lame who come to him there.	1. Jesus comes to the temple as its Lord. He comes to visit and, more than that, to inspect. This is illustrated and elucidated by Jesus' inspection of the fig tree. 2. The temple is God's house, and this is summarized in Jesus' teaching in 11:17. 3. Jesus finds the temple to be barren, just like the fig tree. But this barrenness does not simply mean emptiness, for Jerusalem filled her emptiness with unbelief and disobedience. 4. The temple, including Jerusalem, stands under God's condemnation and judgment. Just as the barren fig tree was cursed and dried up from its roots, so also the temple and the city would be utterly destroyed. 5. Jesus' temple act would be the precipitating event that would ultimately lead to his crucifixion.	The Lucan Jesus is a man of few words and action in the temple incident pericope. He simply drives out the sellers, and then says: "My house shall be called a house of prayer, but you made it a den of robbers" (19:46).	1. The temple incident is placed at the beginning of Jesus' public ministry. 2. The temple is presented as having become a marketplace, and to intensify that claim, John refers to cattle and sheep in addition to the animals listed in the Synoptics. 3. Nonetheless, Jesus expresses ownership and lordship over the temple by calling it "my Father's house." 4. Jesus' protest is quite intense and physical: he uses a whip to drive out the animals. The disciples later associate this and others with the psalmist zeal (Ps 69:9). 5. Jesus' own body is referenced as "the temple," to be destroyed and raised again after three days. 6. Jesus' protest brings him into direct confrontation with the Jewish leaders.

	Matthew	Mark	Luke	John
Its significance in the Gospel's narrative	Matthew's intention for the temple incident pericope is for his readers to see Jesus as the prophesied Davidic Messiah who has authority over and concern for the temple. He expresses that authority and concern not by cursing the temple but by clearing it of sellers and buyers, allowing the blind and the lame into the temple and healing them there, and receiving acclaim from children gathered in the temple precincts who acclaim him as the Son of David.	Mark intends for his readers to see Jesus' temple act as primarily symbolizing God's sovereign and righteous judgment upon the temple for its apparent failure to produce fruits that God had desired. This interpretation is consistent with Mark's sandwiching of the temple incident in the cursing and withering of the fig tree pericope. Jesus' specific actions in the temple—driving out sellers and buyers, overturning tables and chairs, and blockading the passage of goods—should be interpreted not as cleansing but as symbolic of the dissolution of the temple as a result of God's judgment.	Despite the peculiar brevity of the temple incident account, Luke still conveys Jesus' protest at the mercantile activities happening in the temple. He still conveys Jesus lordship over the temple ("my house") and God's condemnation of the Jewish misuse and abuse of the temple. But then Luke does not dwell on that. He moves on to note how the temple becomes the venue of Jesus' daily teaching. Hence, Luke would have intended for his readers to see two things concerning the temple: (1) Luke affirms God's judgment upon the temple, (2) but in spite of that, the temple still serves as a venue for Jesus' teaching and healing activities.	The most significant point that John would have intended for his readers to grasp is that Jesus' own body is the new temple (2:19, 21). This truth would have been very relevant to Jews and non-Jews who lived after 70 CE and had to reckon with the destruction of the temple and the disappearance of institutional Judaism. John's answer to them is, in Carson's words: "It is the human body of Jesus that uniquely manifests the Father, and becomes the focal point of the manifestation of God to man, the living abode of God on earth, the fulfillment of all [that] the temple meant, and the center of all true worship (over against all other claims of 'holy space,' 4:20–24). In this temple the ultimate sacrifice would take place; within three days of death and burial, Jesus Christ, the true temple, would rise again from the dead" (*Gospel*, 182).

The Significance of the Temple Incident in the Narratives of the Four Gospels

In addition to what has been said in the table above, we further note the following conclusions. First, all of the evangelists have indicated Jesus' displeasure (in varying degrees) at, rejection of, or opposition to the mercantile activities that went on in the temple courts. Without exception the evangelists picture Jesus as entering the temple and then driving out the sellers. To interpret Jesus' action as a protest has the *prima facie* support of the text, but to ascertain what Jesus was protesting against is not quite straightforward. Apparently the collective import of the four Gospels allows for a manifold of answers and rule out strait-jacketed dogmatism.

Secondly, despite the diversity in and distinctiveness of the evangelists' literary and theological goals for their own accounts of the incident, common themes and emphases are still apparent, and these may form the integrated significance of Jesus' temple action. These common themes and emphases include Jesus' protest against the commercialization of the temple and the cultus (i.e., the animal sacrifices and the temple tax), Jesus' lordship over the temple, and God's righteous and omnipotent judgment on the temple.

Finally, the question "What is the meaning (understood as *significance*) of Jesus' temple act?" is an ambiguous one and generates endless debates. It needs to be fine-tuned to "What is the *significance* of the temple incident according to, say, Matthew?"

One area for further research is a theology of the temple in the canonical Gospels. This research must consist of a synthetic approach to the four Gospels. This kind of study should begin with what the temple meant for each evangelist and then proceed to a systematic understanding by synthesizing the temple theology of all the four Gospels. Much has already been written on John in relation to this topic.[2] What is lacking is a fair treatment of each evangelist's concept of temple and a synthesis of all their theologies.

---

2. See, for example, Coloe, *God Dwells*; Kerr, *Temple*; Hoskins, *Fulfillment*.

Appendix 1
Summative Comparison of the Four Gospels' Reports of the Temple Incident[1]

Gospel	Matt 21:12–12	Mark 11:15–19	Luke 19:45–46	John 2:13–22
Context	The entry story	The entry story and the cursing of the fig tree	The entry story and the lament over Jerusalem	The wine miracle at Cana
Placement in the Gospel	Towards the end	Towards the end	Towards the end	At the beginning
Location	In the temple	In the temple	In the temple	In the temple
People involved	Jesus, sellers, buyers, money-changers	Jesus, sellers, buyers, money-changers	Jesus, sellers	Jesus, sellers, money-changers
Beasts involved				Oxen, sheep
Birds involved	Pigeons	Pigeons		Pigeons

1. Adapted from Chanikuzhy, *Temple*, 98.

Appendix 1

				Making a whip
	Driving out	Driving out	Driving out	Driving out
				Scattering the coins
	Overturning the tables of the money-changers	Overturning the tables of the money-changers		Overturning the tables of the money-changers
Action of Jesus				Asking the pigeon sellers to take them away
	Overturning the seats of the pigeon sellers	Overturning the seats of the pigeon sellers		
		Prohibiting the carrying of anything through the temple		
Allegation of Jesus	The house of prayer is being made into a den of robbers	The house of prayer for all the nations is being made into a den of robbers	The house of prayer is being made into a den of robbers	His Father's house is being made into a house of trade

Appendix 2
Comparison of the Synoptic Gospels' Accounts of the Temple Incident[1]

Matt 21:12-13	Mark 11:15-19	Luke 19:45-46
	15 καὶ ἔρχονται εἰς Ἱεροσόλυμα	
12 καὶ εἰσῆλθεν Ἰησοῦς εἰς τὸ ἱερόν, καὶ ἐξέβαλεν πάντας τοὺς πωλοῦντας καὶ ἀγοράζοντας ἐν τῷ ἱερῷ,	καὶ εἰσελθὼν εἰς τὸ ἱερὸν ἤρξατο ἐκβάλλειν τοὺς πωλοῦντας καὶ τοὺς ἀγοράζοντας ἐν τῷ ἱερῷ,	45 καὶ εἰσελθὼν εἰς τὸ ἱερὸν ἤρξατο ἐκβάλλειν τοὺς πωλοῦντας
καὶ τὰς τραπέζας τῶν κολλυβιστῶν κατέστρεψεν καὶ τὰς καθέδρας τῶν πωλούντων τὰς περιστεράς,	καὶ τὰς τραπέζας τῶν κολλυβιστῶν καὶ τὰς καθέδρας τῶν πωλούντων τὰς περιστερὰς κατέστρεψεν,	
	16 καὶ οὐκ ἤφιεν ἵνα τις διενέγκῃ σκεῦος διὰ τοῦ ἱεροῦ.	
13 καὶ λέγει αὐτοῖς, Γέγραπται,	17 καὶ ἐδίδασκεν καὶ ἔλεγεν αὐτοῖς, Οὐ γέγραπται ὅτι	46 λέγων αὐτοῖς, Γέγραπται,
Ὁ οἶκός μου οἶκος προσευχῆς κληθήσεται, ὑμεῖς δὲ αὐτὸν ποιεῖτε σπήλαιον λῃστῶν.	Ὁ οἶκός μου οἶκος προσευχῆς κληθήσεται πᾶσιν τοῖς ἔθνεσιν; ὑμεῖς δὲ πεποιήκατε αὐτὸν σπήλαιον λῃστῶν.	Καὶ ἔσται ὁ οἶκός μου οἶκος προσευχῆς, ὑμεῖς δὲ αὐτὸν ἐποιήσατε σπήλαιον λῃστῶν.

1. The Greek texts used here are from the NA[28]. The Gospel of John, being not a Synoptic, is excluded here; it is common knowledge that John differs from the Synoptics on a number of points. See the next appendix.

Appendix 2

	18 καὶ ἤκουσαν οἱ ἀρχιερεῖς καὶ οἱ γραμματεῖς, καὶ ἐζήτουν πῶς αὐτὸν ἀπολέσωσιν· ἐφοβοῦντο γὰρ αὐτόν, πᾶς ὁ ὄχλος ἐξεπλήσσετο ἐπὶ τῇ διδαχῇ αὐτοῦ. (19) καὶ ὅταν ὀψὲ ἐγένετο, ἐξεπορεύοντο ἔξω τῆς πόλεως.	

Appendix 3

Comparison of Mark's and John's Accounts of the Temple Incident[1]

Mark 11:15-19	John 2:13-22
15 καὶ ἔρχονται εἰς Ἱεροσόλυμα	13 καὶ ἐγγὺς ἦν τὸ πάσχα τῶν Ἰουδαίων, καὶ ἀνέβη εἰς Ἱεροσόλυμα ὁ Ἰησοῦς.
καὶ εἰσελθὼν τὸ ἱερὸν ἤρξατο ἐκβάλλειν τοὺς πωλοῦντας καὶ τοὺς ἀγοράζοντας ἐν τῷ ἱερῷ, καὶ τὰς τραπέζας τῶν κολλυβιστῶν καὶ τὰς καθέδρας τῶν πωλούντων τὰς περιστερὰς κατέστρεψεν,	14 καὶ εὗρεν ἐν τῷ ἱερῷ τοὺς πωλοῦντας βόας καὶ πρόβατα καὶ περιστερὰς καὶ τοὺς κερματιστὰς καθημένους, 15 καὶ ποιήσας φραγέλλιον ἐκ σχοινίων πάντας ἐξέβαλεν ἐκ τοῦ ἱεροῦ τά τε πρόβατα καὶ τοὺς βόας, καὶ τῶν κολλυβιστῶν ἐξέχεεν τὰ κέρματα καὶ τὰς τραπέζας ἀνέστρεψεν,
16 καὶ οὐκ ἤφιεν ἵνα τις διενέγκῃ σκεῦος διὰ τοῦ ἱεροῦ.	
17 καὶ ἐδίδασκεν καὶ ἔλεγεν αὐτοῖς, οὐ γέγραπται ὅτι ὁ οἶκός μου οἶκος προσευχῆς κληθήσεται πᾶσιν τοῖς ἔθνεσιν; ὑμεῖς δὲ πεποιήκατε αὐτὸν σπήλαιον λῃστῶν.	16 καὶ τοῖς τὰς περιστερὰς πωλοῦσιν εἶπεν· Ἄρατε ταῦτα ἐντεῦθεν, μὴ ποιεῖτε τὸν οἶκον τοῦ πατρός μου οἶκον ἐμπορίου.
	17 ἐμνήσθησαν οἱ μαθηταὶ αὐτοῦ ὅτι γεγραμμένον ἐστίν· Ὁ ζῆλος τοῦ οἴκου σου καταφάγεταί με.

1. In both Greek and English

Appendix 3

	18 ἀπεκρίθησαν οὖν οἱ Ἰουδαῖοι καὶ εἶπαν αὐτῷ· Τί σημεῖον δεικνύεις ἡμῖν, ὅτι ταῦτα ποιεῖς; 19 ἀπεκρίθη Ἰησοῦς καὶ εἶπεν αὐτοῖς· Λύσατε τὸν ναὸν τοῦτον καὶ ἐν τρισὶν ἡμέραις ἐγερῶ αὐτόν. 20 εἶπαν οὖν οἱ Ἰουδαῖοι· Τεσσεράκοντα καὶ ἓξ ἔτεσιν οἰκοδομήθη ὁ ναὸς οὗτος, καὶ σὺ ἐν τρισὶν ἡμέραις ἐγερεῖς αὐτόν; 21 ἐκεῖνος δὲ ἔλεγεν περὶ τοῦ ναοῦ τοῦ σώματος αὐτοῦ.
18 καὶ ἤκουσαν οἱ ἀρχιερεῖς καὶ οἱ γραμματεῖς, καὶ ἐζήτουν πῶς αὐτόν, πᾶς γὰρ ὁ ὄχλος ἐξεπλήσσετο ἐπὶ τῇ διδαχῇ αὐτοῦ.	22 ὅτε οὖν ἠγέρθη ἐκ νεκρῶν, ἐμνήσθησαν οἱ μαθηταὶ αὐτοῦ ὅτι τοῦτο ἔλεγεν, καὶ ἐπίστευσαν τῇ γραφῇ καὶ τῷ λόγῳ ὃν εἶπεν ὁ Ἰησοῦς.
19 καὶ ὅταν ὀψὲ ἐγένετο, ἐξεπορεύοντο ἔξω τῆς πόλεως.	
15 Then they came to Jerusalem.	13 The Passover of the Jews was near, and Jesus went up to Jerusalem.
And he entered the temple and began to drive out those who were selling and those who were buying in the temple, and he overturned the tables of the money changers and the seats of those who sold doves;	14 In the temple he found people selling cattle, sheep, and doves, and the money changers seated at their tables. 15 Making a whip of cords, he drove all of them out of the temple, both the sheep and the cattle. He also poured out the coins of the money changers and overturned their tables.
16 and he would not allow anyone to carry anything through the temple.	
17 He was teaching and saying, "Is it not written, 'My house shall be called a house of prayer for all the nations'? But you have made it a den of robbers."	16 He told those who were selling the doves, "Take these things out of here! Stop making my Father's house a marketplace!"
	17 His disciples remembered that it was written, "Zeal for your house will consume me."

Comparison of Mark's and John's Accounts of the Temple Incident

18 And when the chief priests and the scribes heard it, they kept looking for a way to kill him; for they were afraid of him, because the whole crowd was spellbound by his teaching.	18 The Jews then said to him, "What sign can you show us for doing this?" 19 Jesus answered them, "Destroy this temple, and in three days I will raise it up." 20 The Jews then said, "This temple has been under construction for forty-six years, and will you raise it up in three days?" 21 But he was speaking of the temple of his body. 22 After he was raised from the dead, his disciples remembered that he had said this; and they believed the scripture and the word that Jesus had spoken.
19 And when evening came, Jesus and his disciples went out of the city.	

Bibliography

Achtemeier, Paul J. "Mark, Gospel of." In *ABD*, 4:541-57.
Alexander, Joseph A. *Commentary on the Gospel According to Mark*. Geneva Series Commentary. Edinburgh: Banner of Truth Trust, 1960.
Alexander, Loveday. "Luke's Preface in the Context of Greek Preface-Writing." *NovT* 28 (1986) 48-74.
―――. *The Preface to Luke's Gospel: Literary Convention and Social Context in Luke 1:1-4 and Acts 1:1*. Society for New Testament Studies Monograph Series 78. Cambridge: Cambridge University Press, 1993.
Allen, Willoughby C. *The Gospel According to Saint Mark: With Introduction and Notes*. London: Rivingtons, 1915.
Anderson, Hugh. *The Gospel of Mark*. New Century Bible. London: Oliphants, 1976.
Ashton, John. *Understanding the Fourth Gospel*. 2nd ed. Oxford: Oxford University Press, 2007.
Bammel, Ernst, and C. F. D. Moule, editors. *Jesus and the Politics of His Day*. Cambridge: Cambridge University Press, 1985.
Barclay, William. *The Gospel of John*. 2 vols. Daily Study Bible Series. Louisville: Westminster John Knox, 1956.
Barrett, C. K. *The Gospel According to St. John: An Introduction with Commentary on the Greek Text*. 2nd ed. Philadelphia: Westminster, 1978.
―――. *Jesus and the Gospel Tradition*. London: SPCK, 1967.
Barth, Gerhard. "Matthew's Understanding of the Law." In *Tradition and Interpretation in Matthew*, edited by Günther Bornkamm et al., 58-164. Philadelphia: Westminster, 1963.
Basser, Herbert W. "Matthew 21:12: Trading Words, Turning the Tables, Timing the End." In *When Judaism and Christianity Began: Essays in Memory of Anthony J. Saldarini*, edited by A. J. Avery-Peck et al., 3-18. Leiden: Brill, 2004.
Bauckham, Richard, editor. "The Beloved Disciple as Ideal Author." *JSNT* 49 (1993) 21-44.
―――. "The Eyewitnesses and the Gospel Traditions." *JSHJ* 1 (2003) 28-60.
―――. *The Gospels for All Christians: Rethinking the Gospel Audiences*. Grand Rapids: Eerdmans, 1998.
―――. "Jesus' Demonstration in the Temple." In *Law and Religion: Essays on the Place of the Law in Israel and Early Christianity*, edited by Barnabas Lindars, 72-89. Cambridge: James Clarke, 1988.
Bauer, David R. *The Structure of Matthew's Gospel: A Study in Literary Design*. Library of New Testament Studies 15. Sheffield: Sheffield Academic, 1989.

Bibliography

Beasley-Murray, G. R. *John*. Word Biblical Commentary 36. Waco, TX: Word, 1987.
Blomberg, Craig L. *The Historical Reliability of the Gospels: Issues and Commentary*. 2nd ed. Downers Grove, IL: InterVarsity, 2007.
Bock, Darrell L. *Luke*. 2 vols. Baker Exegetical Commentary on the New Testament 3A–B. Grand Rapids: Baker, 1994, 1996.
Borchert, Gerald L. *John 1–11: An Exegetical and Theological Exposition of Holy Scripture*. New American Commentary 25A. Nashville: Broadman & Holman, 1996.
Borg, Marcus J. *Jesus: Uncovering the Life, Teachings, and Surprising Relevance of a Spiritual Revolutionary*. New York: Harper and Row, 1994.
Boring, M. Eugene. "The Gospel of Matthew." In *NIB*, 8:89–505.
Borsch, Frederick H. *The Son of Man in Myth and History*. London: SCM, 1967.
Brandon, S. G. F. "The Date of the Markan Gospel." *NTS* 7 (1961) 126–41.
———. *Jesus and the Zealots: A Study of the Political Factor in Primitive Christianity*. Manchester: Manchester University Press, 1967.
Bratcher, Robert G. "A Note on Mark xi.3: ὁ κύριος αὐτοῦ χρείαν ἔχει." *ExpTim* 64 (1952–53) 93.
Brodie, Thomas L. *The Gospel According to John: A Literary and Theological Commentary*. New York: Oxford University Press, 1993.
Brooks, J. A. *Mark*. New American Commentary 23. Nashville: Broadman & Holman, 1991.
Brown, R. E. *The Community of the Beloved Disciple: The Life, Loves and Hates of an Individual Church in New Testament Times*. Mahwah, NJ: Paulist, 1979.
———. *The Gospel According to John: Introduction, Translation, and Notes*. 2 vols. Anchor Bible. Garden City, NY: Doubleday, 1966.
———. *An Introduction to the New Testament*. Anchor Yale Bible Reference Library. New Haven, CT: Yale University Press, 2007.
Brown, Schuyler. *Apostasy and Perseverance in the Theology of Luke*. Analecta Biblica 36. Rome: Pontifical Biblical Institute, 1969.
———. "The Matthean Community and the Gentile Mission." *NovT* 22 (1980) 193–221.
Bruce, F. F. "The Date and Character of Mark." In *Jesus and the Politics of His Day*, edited by Ernst Bammel and C. F. D. Moule, 69–89. Cambridge: Cambridge University Press, 1984.
———. *The Gospel of John: Introduction, Exposition, Notes*. Grand Rapids: Eerdmans, 1994.
Bryan, Steven M. "Consumed by Zeal: John's Use of Psalm 69:9 and the Action in the Temple." *BBR* 21 (2011) 479–94.
Burkett, Delbert. *The Son of Man Debate: A History and Evaluation*. Society for New Testament Studies Monograph Series 107. Cambridge: Cambridge University Press, 2004.
Cadbury, H. J. "Commentary on the Preface of Luke." In *The Beginnings of Christianity*, edited by F. J. Foakes Jackson and K. Lake, 1:489–510. London: Macmillan, 1922.
Callan, Terrance. "The Preface of Luke–Acts and Historiography." *NTS* 31 (1985) 576–81.
Carson, D. A. *The Gospel According to John*. Grand Rapids: Eerdmans, 1991.
———. "The Purpose of the Fourth Gospel: John 20:30–31 Reconsidered." *JBL* 108 (1987) 639–51.
Carson, D. A. and Douglas J. Moo. *An Introduction to the New Testament*. Grand Rapids: Zondervan, 2005.

Bibliography

Casey, Maurice. *Aramaic Sources of Mark's Gospel*. Cambridge: Cambridge University Press, 1998.
Chance, J. Bradley. *Jerusalem, the Temple, and the New Age in Luke-Acts*. Macon, GA: Mercer University Press, 1988.
Chanikuzhy, Jacob. *Jesus, the Eschatological Temple: An Exegetical Study of Jn 2:13– 22 in the Light of the Pre-70 C.E. Eschatological Temple Hopes and the Synoptic Gospel Traditions*. Contributions to Biblical Exegesis and Theology. Leuven: Peeters, 2012.
Collins, Adela Yarbro. "Jesus' Action in Herod's Temple." In *Antiquity and Humanity: Essays on Ancient Religion and Philosophy, Presented to Hanz Dieter Betz on His Seventieth Birthday*, edited by A. Y. Collins and M. M. Mitchell, 45–61. Tübingen: Mohr Siebeck, 2001.
Collins, Raymond F. *These Things Have Been Written: Studies on the Fourth Gospel*. Louvain Theological and Pastoral Monographs 2. Louvain: Peeters, 1990.
Coloe, Mary L. *God Dwells with Us: Temple Symbolism in the Fourth Gospel*. Collegeville, MN: Liturgical Press, 2001.
———. "Temple Imagery in John." *Int* 63 (2009) 368–81.
Congar, Yves M.-J. *The Mystery of the Temple*. Westminster, MD: Newman, 1958.
Conzelmann, Hans. *An Outline of the Theology of the New Testament*. Translated by J. S. Bowden. London: SCM, 1969.
———. *The Theology of St. Luke*. Translated by G. Buswell. London: Faber and Faber, 1961.
Cranfield, C. E. B. *The Gospel According to Saint Mark*. Cambridge Greek Testament Commentary. Cambridge: Cambridge University Press, 1963.
Crossan, John Dominic. "Redaction and Citation in Mark 11:9–10 and 11:17." *BR* 17 (1972) 33–50.
Crossley, James G. *The Date of Mark's Gospel: Insight from the Law in Earliest Christianity*. London: T&T Clark, 2004.
Croy, N. Clayton. "The Messianic Whippersnapper: Did Jesus Use a Whip on People in the Temple (John 2:15)?" *JBL* 128 (2009) 555–68.
Cullmann, Oscar. *The Johannine Circle*. Translated by John Bowden. Philadelphia: Westminster John Knox, 1976.
Culpepper, R. Alan. *The Gospel and Letters of John*. Interpreting Biblical Texts. Nashville: Abingdon, 2008.
———. *The Johannine School: An Evaluation of the Johannine-School Hypothesis Based on an Investigation of the Nature of Ancient Schools*. Society of Biblical Literature Dissertation Series 26. Missoula, MT: Scholars Press, 1975.
———. *Mark*. Smyth and Helwys Bible Commentary. Macon, GA: Smyth & Helwys, 2007.
Danker, Frederick W. *Jesus and the New Age: A Commentary on St. Luke's Gospel*. Philadelphia: Fortress, 1988.
Davies, Brian, editor. *Language, Meaning, and God: Essays in Honor of Herbert McCabe, OP*. London: Geoffrey Chapman, 1987.
Davies, W. D. *The Setting of the Sermon on the Mount*. Cambridge: Cambridge University Press, 1966.
Davies, W. D., and D. C. Allison. *Matthew*. 3 vols. International Critical Commentary. Edinburgh: T&T Clark, 1988–97.
Dawsey, J. M. "Confrontation in the Temple: Luke 1945–20:47." *PRSt* 11 (1984) 153–65.
Derrett, J. D. M. "Law in the NT: The Palm Sunday Colt." *NovT* 13 (1971) 241–58.

Bibliography

Dillon, R. J. "Previewing Luke's Project from His Prologue (Luke 1:1–4)." *CBQ* 43 (1981) 205–27.

Dodd, C. H. *Historical Tradition in the Fourth Gospel*. Cambridge: Cambridge University Press, 1963.

Donahue, John R., and Daniel J. Harrington. *The Gospel of Mark*. Sacra Pagina Series 2. Collegeville, MN: Liturgical Press, 2002.

Duff, Paul B. "The March of the Divine Warrior and the Advent of the Greco-Roman King: Mark's Account of Jesus' Entry into Jerusalem." *JBL* 111 (1992) 55–71.

Duling, D. C. *The Interpretation of the Fourth Gospel*. Cambridge: Cambridge University Press, 1953.

———. "The Therapeutic Son of David: An Element in Matthew's Christological Apologetic." *NTS* 24 (1978) 392–410.

Edersheim, Alfred. *The Life and Times of Jesus the Messiah*. Rev. ed. Peabody, MA: Hendrickson, 1993.

Edwards, James R. *The Gospel According to Mark*. Pillar New Testament Commentary. Grand Rapids: Eerdmans, 2002.

Ellis, E. Earle. "The Date and Provenance of Mark's Gospel." In *The Four Gospels 1992: Festschrift Frans Neirynck*, edited by F. Segbroecket al., 801–15. Bibliotheca Ephemeridum Theologicarum Lovaniensium 100. Leuven: Leuven University Press, 1992.

———. *The Gospel of Luke*. Century Bible. London: Nelson, 1966.

Evans, Craig A. "'The Book of the Genesis of Jesus Christ': The Purpose of Matthew in Light of the Incipit." In *The Gospel of Matthew*, edited by T. R. Hatina, 61–72. Vol. 2 of *Biblical Interpretation in Early Christian Gospels*. New York: T&T Clark, 2008.

———. "Jesus' Action in the Temple: Cleansing or Portent of Destruction?" *CBQ* 51 (1989) 237–70.

———. *Luke*. Understanding the Bible Commentary 3. Peabody, MA: Hendrickson, 1990.

———. *Mark 8:27—16:20*. Word Biblical Commentary 34B. Nashville: Nelson, 2001.

Fay, Ron C. "The Narrative Function of the Temple in Luke-Acts." *TJ* (1996) 255–70.

Fee, Gordon D. "On the Text and Meaning of John 20:30–31." In *The Four Gospels 1992: Festschrift Frans Neirynck*, edited by F. Van Segbroeck et al., 2193–2205. Bibliotheca Ephemeridum Theologicarum Lovaniensium 3. Leuven: Leuven University Press, 1992.

———. "The Use of the Definite Article with Proper Names in the Gospel of John." *NTS* 17 (1970–71) 168–83.

Fitzmyer, Joseph A. "Aramaic Evidence Affecting the Interpretation of *Hosanna* in the New Testament." In *Tradition and interpretation in the New Testament: Essays in Honor of E. Earle Ellis for his 60th Birthday*, edited by G. F. Hawthorne and O. Betz, 110–18. Grand Rapids: Eerdmans, 1987.

———. *The Gospel According to Luke: Introduction, Translation, and Notes*. 2 vols. Anchor Bible 28. Garden City, NY: Doubleday, 1982–85.

Ford, J. M. "Money 'Bags' in the Temple (Mark 11:16)." *Bib* 57 (1976) 249–53.

France, R. T. "Chronological Aspects of 'Gospel Harmony.'" *VE* 16 (1986) 33–59.

———. *The Gospel of Mark*. The New International Greek Testament Commentary. Grand Rapids: Eerdmans, 2002.

———. *The Gospel of Matthew*. The New International Greek Testament Commentary. Grand Rapids: Eerdmans, 2007.

Bibliography

———. *Matthew: Evangelist and Teacher.* London: Paternoster, 1989.
Fredriksen, Paula. "Gospel Chronologies, the Scene at the Temple, and the Crucifixion of Jesus." In *Redefining First-Century Jewish Identities: Essays in Honor of Ed Parish Sanders,* edited by Fabian E. Udoh, 246-82. Notre Dame: University of Notre Dame Press, 2008.
Fuller, R. H. *The Foundations of New Testament Christology.* London: Lutterworth, 1965.
Glancy, Jennifer A. "Violence as a Sign in the Fourth Gospel." *BibInt* 17 (2009) 100-117.
Goulder, M. D. *Luke.* Journal for the Study of the New Testament Supplement Series 20. Sheffield: Sheffield Academic, 1989.
———. *Midrash and Lection in Matthew.* London: SPCK, 1974.
Gray, Timothy C. *The Temple in the Gospel of Mark: A Study in Its Narrative Role.* Wissenschaftliche Untersuchungen zum Neuen Testament 2/242. Tübingen: Mohr Siebeck, 2008.
Guelich, R. A. *Mark 1-8.* Word Biblical Commentary 26. Dallas: Word, 1989.
Gundry, Robert H. *Mark: A Commentary for His Apology for the Cross.* Grand Rapids: Eerdmans, 1993.
———. *Matthew: A Commentary on His Handbook for a Mixed Church under Persecution.* 2nd ed. Grand Rapids: Eerdmans, 1994.
Guthrie, Donald.. *New Testament Introduction.* 4th ed. Downers Grove, IL: InterVarsity, 1990.
Haenchen, Ernst. *A Commentary on the Gospel of John.* 2 vols. Translated by R. W. Funk. Edited by R. W. Funk and U. Busse. Philadelphia: Fortress, 1984.
Hagner, D. A. *Matthew 1-13.* Word Biblical Commentary 33A. Dallas: Word, 1993.
Hahn, Ferdinand. *The Titles of Jesus in Christology.* London: Lutterworth, 1969.
Harnack, Adolf. *Date of the Acts and the Synoptic Gospels.* London: Williams & Norgate, 1911.
Harrington, Daniel J. *The Gospel of Matthew.* Sacra Pagina 1. Collegeville, MN: Liturgical Press, 1991.
Hendriksen, William. *Exposition of the Gospel According to John.* 2 vols. Grand Rapids: Baker, 1953-54.
Hengel, Martin. *The Johannine Question.* Translated by John Bowden. London: SCM, 1989.
———. *Studies in the Gospel of Mark.* Philadelphia: Fortress, 1985.
Higgins, A. J. B. *The Son of Man in the Teaching of Jesus.* Society for New Testament Studies Monograph Series 39. Cambridge: Cambridge University Press, 1980.
Hood, Jason B. *The Messiah, His Brothers, and the Nations (Matthew 1:1-17).* Library of New Testament Studies 441. New York: T&T Clark, 2011.
Hooker, Morna D. *A Commentary on the Gospel According to St. Mark.* Black's New Testament Commentaries. London: Black, 1991.
Horsley, Richard A. *Bandits, Prophets, and Messiahs: Popular Movements in the Time of Jesus.* Harrisburg, PA: Trinity, 1999.
Hoskins, Paul M. *Jesus as the Fulfillment of the Temple in the Gospel of John.* Paternoster Biblical Monographs. Eugene, OR: Wipf & Stock, 2006.
Hummel, Reinhart. *Die Auseinandersetzung zwischen Kirche und Judentum im Matthäusevangelium.* 2nd ed. Beiträge zur evangelischen Theologie 33. Munich: Kaiser, 1966.
Hurtado, Larry W. *Mark.* New International Biblical Commentary. Peabody, MA: Hendrickson, 1989.

Bibliography

Juel, Donald. *Messiah and Temple: The Trial of Jesus in the Gospel of Mark*. Society of Biblical Literature Dissertation Series 31. Missoula, MT: Scholars Press, 1977.
Keener, Craig S. *The Gospel of John: A Commentary*. 2 vols. Peabody, MA: Hendrickson, 2003.
———. *The IVP Bible Background Commentary*. Downers Grove, IL: InterVarsity Press, 1993.
Kelber, W. H. *The Kingdom of God: A New Place and a New Time*. Philadelphia: Fortress, 1974.
Kerr, Alan R. *The Temple of Jesus' Body: The Temple Theme in the Gospel of John*. Journal for the Study of the New Testament Supplement Series 220. Sheffield: Sheffield Academic, 2002.
Kingsbury, J. D. *Matthew: Structure, Christology, and Kingdom*. Philadelphia: Fortress, 1975.
———. *Matthew as Story*. 2nd ed. Philadelphia: Fortress, 1988.
Kinman, Brent. *Jesus' Entry into Jerusalem: In the Context of Lucan Theology and the Politics of His Day*. Arbeiten zur Geschichte des antiken Judentums und des Urchristentums 28. Leiden: Brill, 1995.
———. "Jesus' Royal Entry into Jerusalem." *BBR* 15 (2005) 223–60.
———. "Parousia, Jesus' 'A-Triumphal' Entry, and the Fate of Jerusalem (Luke 19:28–44)." *JBL* 118 (1999) 279–94.
Knight, Jonathan. *Luke's Gospel*. New Testament Readings. London: Routledge, 1998.
Koester, Craig R. *Symbolism in the Fourth Gospel: Meaning, Mystery, and Community*. Minneapolis: Fortress, 1995.
Köstenberger, Andreas J. "'The Disciple Jesus Loved': Witness, Author, Apostle—A Response to Richard Bauckham's *Jesus and the Eyewitness*." *BBR* (18) 209–31.
Köstenberger, Andreas J., and Richard D. Patterson. *Invitation to Biblical Interpretation: Exploring the Hermeneutical Triad of History, Literature, and Theology*. Grand Rapids: Kregel, 2011.
Köstenberger, Andreas J., et al. *The Cradle, the Cross, and the Crown: An Introduction to the New Testament*. Nashville: B. & H., 2009.
Kruse, Colin G. *John: An Introduction and Commentary*. Tyndale New Testament Commentaries. Downers Grove, IL: InterVarsity Press, 2003.
Kümmel, W. G. *Introduction to the New Testament*. Translated by H. C. Kee. Nashville: Abingdon, 1975.
Lane, William L. *The Gospel of Mark*. New International Commentary on the New Testament. Grand Rapids: Eerdmans, 1974.
Lasserre, Jean. "A Tenacious Misinterpretation: John 2:15." Translated by John H. Yoder. In *Occasional Papers of the Council of Mennonite Seminaries and Institute of Mennonite Studies 1*, edited by W. M. Swartley. Elkhart, IN: Institute of Mennonite Studies, 1981.
Levin, Yigal. "Jesus, 'Son of God' and 'Son of David': The 'Adoption' of Jesus into the Davidic Line." *JSNT* 28 (2006) 415–42.
Licona, Michael R. *Why Are There Differences in the Gospels? What We Can Learn from Ancient Biography*. Oxford: Oxford University Press, 2017.
Liefeld, W. L. "Luke." In *EBC* 10:19–356.
Lightfoot, R. H. *The Gospel Message of St. Mark*. Oxford: Clarendon, 1950.
———. "Unsolved New Testament Problems: The Cleansing of the Temple in St. John's Gospel." *ExpTim* 60 (1948) 64–68.

Lincoln, Andrew T. *The Gospel According to St. John*. Black's New Testament Commentaries. London: Continuum, 2005.

Lindars, Barnabas. *The Gospel of John*. New Century Bible Commentary. London: Marshall, Morgan & Scott; Grand Rapids: Eerdmans, 1972.

Loader, W. R. G. "Son of David, Blindness, Possession, and Duality in Matthew." *CBQ* 44 (1982) 570–85.

Maas, Anthony. "Chronology of the Life of Jesus Christ." *The Catholic Encyclopedia*. Vol. 8. New York: Robert Appleton, 1910. http://www.newadvent.org/cathen/08377a.htm.

Mack, Burton L. *A Myth of Innocence: Mark and Christian Origins*. Philadelphia: Fortress, 1988.

Maddox, Robert. *The Purpose of Luke-Acts*. Forschungen zur Religion und Literatur des Alten und Neuen Testaments 126. Göttingen: Vandenhoeck & Ruprecht. Reprinted, Edinburgh: T&T Clark, 1982.

Manson, T. W. "The Cleansing of the Temple." *BJRL* 33 (1951) 271–82.

Marcus, Joel. "The Jewish War and the *Sitz im Leben* of Mark." *JBL* 111 (1992) 441–62.

———. *Mark 1–8: A New Translation with Introduction and Commentary*. Anchor Bible Reference Library 27. New York: Doubleday, 2000.

———. *The Way of the Lord: Christological Exegesis of the Old Testament in the Gospel of Mark*. London: T&T Clark, 2004.

Marshall, I. Howard. *The Gospel of Luke*. The New International Greek Testament Commentary. Grand Rapids: Eerdmans, 1978.

———. *Luke: Historian and Theologian*. New Testament Profiles. Downers Grove, IL: InterVarsity, 1998.

Matson, M. A. "The Contribution to the Temple Cleansing by the Fourth Gospel." In *Society of Biblical Literature 1992 Seminar Papers*, edited by E. H. Lovering, 145–53. Atlanta: Scholars Press, 1992.

Matthews, Kenneth A. "John, Jesus, and the Essenes: Trouble at the Temple." *CTR* 3 (1988) 101–26.

McGrath, James F. "'Destroy This Temple': Issues of History in John 2:13–22." In *John, Jesus, and History: Aspects of Historicity in the Fourth Gospel*, edited by Paul N. Anderson et al., 2:35–43. Society of Biblical Literature Symposium Series 44. Atlanta: SBL Press, 2009.

Meier, John P. *The Vision of Matthew: Christ, Church, and Morality in the First Gospel*. New York: Crossroad, 1991.

Metzger, Bruce M. *A Textual Commentary on the Greek New Testament*. 2nd ed. Stuttgart: Deutsche Bibelgesellschaft, 1994.

Michaels, J. Ramsey. *John*. New International Commentary on the New Testament. Peabody, MA: Hendrickson, 1989.

Milne, Bruce. *The Message of John*. The Bible Speaks Today. Downers Grove, IL: InterVarsity Press, 1993.

Moloney, Frank J. *The Gospel of John*. Sacra Pagina 4. Collegeville, MN: Liturgical Press, 1998.

———. "Reading John 2:13–22: The Purification of the Temple." *RB* 90 (1990) 432–52.

Moore, Stephen D. *Literary Criticism and the Gospels: The Theoretical Challenge*. New Haven, CT: Yale University Press, 1989.

Moritz, T. "Mark, Book of." In *Dictionary for Theological Interpretation of the Bible*, edited by Kevin J. Vanhoozer, 480–84. Grand Rapids: Baker, 2005.

Bibliography

Morris, Leon. *The Gospel According to John*. New International Commentary on the New Testament. Grand Rapids: Eerdmans, 1995.

———. *The Gospel According to St. Luke: An Introduction and Commentary*. Tyndale New Testament Commentaries. Grand Rapids: Eerdmans, 1988.

Moulton, H. K. "*Pantas* in John 2:15." *BT* 18 (1967) 126–27.

Mullins, T. Y. "Jesus, the 'Son of David.'" *AUSS* 29 (1991) 117–26.

Myers, Ched. *Binding the Strong Man: A Political Reading of Mark's Story of Jesus*. Maryknoll, NY: Orbis, 1988.

Nereparampil, L. *Destroy This Temple: An Exegetico-Theological Study on the Meaning of Jesus' Temple-Logion in Jn 2:19*. Bangalore: Dharmaram College, 1978.

Neufeld, Thomas R. Yoder. *Killing Enmity: Violence and the New Testament*. Grand Rapids: Baker, 2011.

Nolland, John. *Luke 18:35–24:53*. Word Biblical Commentary 35C. Dallas: Word, 1993.

———. *The Gospel of Matthew*. New International Greek Testament Commentary. Grand Rapids: Eerdmans, 2005.

Novakovic, Lidija. *Messiah: The Healer of the Sick*. Wissenschaftliche Untersuchungen zum Neuen Testament 2/170. Tübingen: Mohr Siebeck, 2003.

Oden, Thomas C., and Christopher A. Hall, editors. *Mark*. Ancient Christian Commentary on Scripture: New Testament 2. Downers Grove, IL: InterVarsity Press, 1998.

O'Toole, Robert F. *The Unity of Luke's Theology: An Analysis of Luke-Acts*. Wilmington, DE: Glazier, 1984.

Overman, J. A. *Matthew's Gospel and Formative Judaism: The Social World of the Matthean Community*. Philadelphia: Fortress, 1990.

Painter, John. "The Point of John's Christology: Christology, Conflict and Community in John." In *Christology, Controversy, and Community: New Testament Essays in Honour of David R. Catchpole*, edited by D. G. Horrell and C. M. Tuckett. Supplements to Novum Testamentum 99. Leiden: Brill, 2000.

———. *The Quest for the Messiah: The History, Literature, and Theology of the Johannine Community*. 2nd ed. Nashville: Abingdon, 1993.

Perkins, Pheme. "The Gospel of Mark: Introduction, Commentary, and Reflections." In *NIB* 8:503–733.

Perschbacher, W. J. *The New Analytical Greek Lexicon*. Peabody, MA: Hendrickson, 1990.

Pitre, Brant. "Jesus, the New Temple, and the New Priesthood." *L&S* 4 (2008) 47–83.

Plutarch. *Antonius*. Translated by Bernadotte Perrin. LCL. Cambridge, MA: Harvard University Press, 1920.

Porter, Stanley E., and Andrew W. Pitts, editors. *Christian Origins and Greco-Roman Culture: Social and Literary Contexts for the New Testament*. Text and Editions for New Testament Study 9. Leiden: Brill, 2013.

Prins, E. J. "The Messiah, Son of David: An Inquiry into Mark 12:35–37." Master's thesis, Utrecht University, 2009.

Qualls, P. F. "Mark 11:15–18: A Prophetic Challenge." *RevExp* 93 (1996) 395–402.

Radcliffe, Timothy. "The Coming of the Son of Man: Mark's Gospel and the Subversion of the Apocalyptic Imagination." In *Language, Meaning and God: Essays in Honor of Herbert McCabe, OP*, edited by Brian Davies, 176–89. London: G. Chapman, 1987.

Repschinski, Boris. *The Controversy Stories in the Gospel of Matthew: Their Redaction, Form, and Relevance for the Relationship Between the Matthean Community and Formative Judaism*. Forschungen zur Religion und Literatur des Alten und Neuen Testaments 189. Göttingen: Vandenhoeck & Ruprecht, 2000.

Richardson, Peter. "Why Turn the Tables? Jesus' Protest in the Temple Precincts." In *Society of Biblical Literature 1992 Seminar Papers*, edited by E. H. Lovering, 507–23. Society of Biblical Literature Seminar Papers 31. Atlanta: Scholars Press, 1992.

Robbins, V. K. (1979). "Preface in Greco-Roman Biography and Luke-Acts." *PRSt* 6 (1979) 94–108.

Robinson, J. A. T. *The Priority of John.* London: SCM, 1985.

———. *Redating the New Testament.* London: SCM, 1976.

Saldarini, Anthony J. *Matthew's Christian-Jewish Community.* Chicago Studies in the History of Judaism. Chicago: University of Chicago Press, 1994.

———. "Scribes." In *ABD* 5:1012–16.

Sanders, E. P. *Jesus and Judaism.* Philadelphia: Fortress, 1985.

Sanders, E. P., and Margaret Davies. *Studying the Synoptic Gospels.* London: SCM, 1989.

Schnackenburg, Rudolf. *The Gospel According to St. John: Introduction, and Commentary on Chapters 1–4.* New York: Crossroad, 1980.

Schnelle, Udo. *Theology of the New Testament.* Translated by M. Eugene Boring. Grand Rapids: Baker, 2007.

Schröter, Jens. "The Gospel of Mark." In *The Blackwell Companion to the New Testament*, edited by David Aune, 272–95. Oxford: Blackwell, 2010.

Schwarz, Hans. *Eschatology.* Grand Rapids: Eerdmans, 2000.

Senior, Donald. "The New Testament and Peacemaking: Some Problem Passages. *FM* 4 (1986) 71–7.

———. "'With Swords and Clubs . . .'—The Setting of Mark's Community and His Critique of Abusive Power." *BTB* 17 (1987) 10–20.

Sim, David C. *The Gospel of Matthew and Christian Judaism: The History and Social Setting of the Matthean Community.* Edinburgh: T&TClark, 1998.

Smith, C. W. F. "No Time for Figs." *JBL* 79 (1960) 315–27.

———. "Tabernacles in the Fourth Gospel and Mark." *NTS* 9 (1963) 130–46.

Song, Young-Mog. *The Eschatological Exodus Theme in the Three Canticles in Luke 1–2.* ThM thesis, Potchefstroom University for Christian Higher Education, 1999.

———. "The Prophetic Identity of Jesus in *Pericope de Aulterae* (John 7:53–8:11)." *KENTS* 12 (2013) 545.

Stein, R. H. *Luke.* New American Commentary 24. Nashville: B&H Publishing, 1992.

———. *Mark.* Baker Exegetical Commentary on the New Testament. Grand Rapids: Baker, 2008.

Stendahl, Krister. *The School of St. Matthew and Its Use of the Old Testament.* 2nd ed. Philadelphia: Fortress, 1968.

Stibbe, M. W. G. *John's Gospel.* New Testament Readings. London: Routledge, 1994.

Strauss, Mark L. *The Davidic Messiah in Luke-Acts: The Promise and Its Fulfillment in Lukan Christology.* Journal for the Study of the New Testament Supplement Series 110. Sheffield: Sheffield Academic, 1995.

Strecker, Georg. "The Concept of History in Matthew." In *The Interpretation of Matthew*, edited by Graham Stanton, 81–100. Philadelphia: Fortress, 1983.

Swartley, William M. *Covenant of Peace: The Missing Peace in New Testament Theology and Ethics.* Grand Rapids: Eerdmans, 2006.

Tan, Randall. "Recent Developments in Redaction Criticism: From Investigation of Textual Prehistory Back to Historical-Grammatical Exegesis?" *JETS* 44 (2001) 599–614.

Bibliography

Tannehill, R. C. *Luke*. Abingdon New Testament Commentaries. Nashville: Abingdon, 1996.

———. *The Narrative Unity of Luke-Acts: A Literary Interpretation*. Vol. 1, *The Gospel According to Luke*. Philadelphia: Fortress, 1986.

Tatum, W. Barnes. "Jesus' So-Called Triumphal Entry: On Making an Ass with the Romans. *Forum* 1 (1998) 129–43.

Taylor, Vincent. *The Gospel According to St. Mark*. London: Macmillan, 1966.

Teeple, H. M. "Origin of the Son of Man Christology." *JBL* 84 (1965) 213–50.

Telford, William. R. *The Barren Temple and the Withered Tree*. Journal for the Study of the New Testament Supplement Series 1. Sheffield: JSOT Press, 1980.

———. *Mark*. Sheffield: Sheffield University Press, 1996.

———. *The Theology of the Gospel of Mark*. Cambridge: Cambridge University Press, 1999.

Theissen, Gerd. *The Gospels in Context: Social and Political History in the History of the Synoptic Gospels*. Translated by Linda M. Maloney. Edinburgh: T. & T. Clark, 1992.

Thiede, Carsten P. *The Earliest Gospel Manuscript? The Qumran Fragment 7Q5 and Its Significance for New Testament Studies*. Exeter: Paternoster, 1992.

Tiede, David L. *Prophecy and History in Luke-Acts*. Philadelphia: Fortress, 1980.

Tödt, Heinz E. *The Son of Man in the Synoptic Tradition*. London: SCM, 1965.

Torrey, Charles Cutler. *Documents of the Primitive Church*. New York: Harper, 1941.

Toussaint, Stanley. D. "The Significance of the First Sign in John's Gospel." *BibSac* 134 (1977) 45–51.

Twelftree, Graham H. *Jesus the Miracle Worker: A Historical and Theological Study*. Downers Grove, IL: InterVarsity, 1999.

Unger, Merrill F. *The New Unger's Bible Dictionary*. Rev. 3rd ed. Chicago: Moody, 1996.

Vanhoozer, Kevin J., editor. *Dictionary for Theological Interpretation of the Bible*. Grand Rapids: Baker, 2005.

Van Iersel, Bas M. F. "Failed Followers in Mark: Mark 13:12 as a Key for the Identification of the Intended Readers." *CBQ* 58 (1996) 244–63.

———. *Mark: A Reader-Response Commentary*. Translated by W. H. Bisscheroux. Sheffield: Sheffield Academic, 1998.

Vistar, Deolito V., Jr. "The Supreme Σημεῖον of Jesus' Death-and-Resurrection in the Fourth Gospel." PhD diss., University of Otago, 2018. https://ourarchive.otago.ac.nz/handle/10523/7881.

———. *The Cross-and-Resurrection: The Supreme Σημεῖον in the Fourth Gospel*. WUNT 2. Tübingen: Mohr Siebeck, forthcoming.

Walker, P. W. L. *Jesus and the Holy City: New Testament Perspectives on Jerusalem*. Grand Rapids: Eerdmans, 1996.

Watts, Rikki E. *Isaiah's New Exodus in Mark*. Tübingen: Mohr (Siebeck), 1997.

———. "Mark." In *Commentary on the New Testament Use of the Old Testament*, edited by G. K. Beale and D. A. Carson, 111–250. Grand Rapids: Baker, 2007.

Weinert, F. D. "Luke, the Temple and Jesus' Saying about Jerusalem's Abandoned House (Luke 13:34–35)." *CBQ* 44 (1982) 68–76.

———. "Luke, Stephen, and the Temple in Luke-Acts." *BTB* 17 (1987) 88–90.

———. "The Meaning of the Temple in Luke-Acts." *BTB* 11 (1981) 85–89.

Wenham, John W. *Redating Matthew, Mark and Luke*. London: Hodder & Stoughton, 1991.

Whitacre, R. A. *John*. New Testament Commentaries 4. Downers Grove, IL: InterVarsity Press, 1999.
Willitts, Joel. *Matthew's Messianic Shepherd-King: In Search of "the Lost Sheep of the House of Israel."* Beihafte zur Zeitschrift für neutestamentliche Wissenschaft 147. Berlin: de Gruyter, 2007.
Winn, Adam. *The Purpose of Mark's Gospel: An Early Christian Response to Roman Imperial Propaganda*. Wissenschaftliche Untersuchungen zum Neuen Testament 2/245. Tübingen: Mohr Siebeck, 2008.
Witherington, Ben, III. *The Gospel of Mark: A Socio-Rhetorical Commentary*. Grand Rapids: Eerdmans, 2001.
———. *John's Wisdom: A Commentary on the Fourth Gospel*. Louisville: Westminster John Knox, 1995.
Wohlgemut, Joel R. "Where Does God Dwell? A Commentary on John 2:13–22." *Direction* 22 (1993) 87–93.
Wong, Solomon Hon-Fai. *The Temple Incident in Mark 11, 15–19*. New Testament Studies in Contextual Exegesis 5. Frankfurt: Peter Lang, 2009.
Wrede, William. *The Messianic Secret*. Translated by J. C. Greig. London: James Clarke, 1971.
Wright, N. T. *Jesus and the Victory of God*. Christian Origins and the Question of God 2. Minneapolis: Fortress, 1996.
———. *The New Testament and the People of God*. Christian Origins and the Question of God 1. Minneapolis: Fortress, 1992.
Wright, S. I. "Luke, Book of." In *Dictionary for Theological Interpretation of the Bible*, edited by Kevin J. Vanhoozer, 467–71. Grand Rapids: Baker, 2005.
Yarbrough, R. W. "The Date of Papias: A Reassessment." *JETS* 26 (1983) 181–91.
Zahn, Theodore B. *Introduction to the New Testament*. 3 vols. Edinburgh: T&T Clark, 1909.

Index of Subjects

Anti-Marcionite Prologue, 34–36, 65

beloved disciple, 85–86
Birkath ha-Minim, 9

Clement of Alexandria, 31–32, 35, 36
composition criticism, 3–4
Council of Jamnia, 10
Court of the Gentiles, 21–22, 102

discipleship, 38

entry into Jerusalem
    Matthean, 14–18
    Marcan, 41–51
    Lucan, 71–76
Eusebius, 31–32, 34–36, 65

fulfillment of Scripture, 11–12, 14–15,
    28, 62, 69, 74, 76

Hallel Psalms, 45
healing in the temple, 17–20

Irenaeus, 31, 34, 36, 65

Jamnia, Council of, 10
Justin Martyr, 31, 34, 35, 65

King of Israel, 17, 42, 102
King of the Jews, 16
kingship, Jesus', 46, 73, 75, 80

Lamb of God, 102

Messiah, 3, 8, 12, 15–17, 19, 21, 25, 26,
    28, 42, 51, 55, 62, 73
messianism, 50, 74, 80
Muratorian Canon, 32, 65

Nero, 35–37

Origen, 32, 35

Papias, 31–34
Papyrus Bodmer XIV, 65
Passover, 13, 17, 23, 47, 56, 101–103
Peter, 33, 35
public ministry, Jesus', 13

Qumran Community, 18

Signs, Johannine, 92, 108
Son of David, 3, 16–19, 21, 42–43, 51
Son of Man, 42, 102

temple incident
    Matthean, 21–28
    Marcan, 53–61
    Lucan, 71–76
    Johannine, 98–110
Tertullian, 31
Theophilus, 67–68

wine miracle in Cana, 91–96
Wrede, William, 33–34

Index of Greek Words and Phrases

ἀγγαρεία, 49, 50
ἀποσυνάγωγος, 88

βασιλεύς, 74

γράφω, 11n20, 25

δεῖ, 69
δύναμις, 19

ἐκβάλλω, 22
ἐκπορεύομαι, 54n100
ἐκ σχοινίων, 104

θαυμασία, 19

ἱερόν, 21, 45–46, 102, 110n93
Ἰουδαῖοι, 108

κύκλος, 77
κύριος, 49, 73

λῃστής, 27
λόγος, 102, 110

ναός, 102, 109–110

ὁ ἐρχόμενος, 50, 75
οἱ ἀρχιερεῖς, 57
οἱ γραμματεῖς, 57
οἱ πρεσβύτεροι, 57

πάντας, 104, 105
πᾶσιν τοῖς ἔθνεσιν, 58, 62
πιστεύειν, 87
πληρόω, 11n20

σημεῖον, 108
σκεῦος, 56, 59
σπήλαιον λῃστῶν, 27, 28
στιβάς, 44
συνέχειν, 77
σῴζω, 69n20
σωτηρία, 69n20
σωτήριον, 69n20
σωτήρ, 69n20

φραγγέλιον, 104

χαράξ, 77

ὥρα, 94
ὡσάννα, 44, 45

Index of Authors

Achtemeier, Paul J., 31n3
Alexander, Joseph A., 48n72, 50, 66n9, 67n11
Allison, Dale C., 1n4, 16n36, 17n42, 19n52, 21, 22n62
Anderson, Hugh, 48, 50, 57
Ashton, John, 93n33, 94

Barclay, William, 94
Barrett, C. K., 42n49, 99, 104
Barth, Gerhard, 9n9
Bauckham, Richard, 9n6, 23n64, 23n65, 23n66, 24, 26, 59n119, 85n6
Bauer, David R., 12
Beasley-Murray, G. R., 87n18, 100n59
Blomberg, Craig L., 85n5, 86n12
Bock, Darrell L., 1n4, 66n8, 67n14, 68, 75n32, 77n37, 80n44
Borchert, Gerald L., 98n50
Borg, Marcus J., 23n66, 25n70,
Boring, M. Eugene, 25n72
Borsch, Frederick H., 42n49
Brandon, S. G. F., 58n113
Bratcher, Robert G., 44n55
Brooks, J. A., 31n3, 32
Brown, Raymond E., 1n4, 37n33, 40n44, 65n5, 66n9, 85n4, 93n33, 100, 104
Brown, Schuyler, 9n9
Bruce, F. F., 85n5
Burkett, Delbert, 42n48

Cadbury, H. J., 66n9
Callan, Terrance, 66n9

Carson, D. A., 1n4, 9n8, 32, 35, 36, 37n34, 66, 67nn12–13, 70n22, 85n5, 86n15, 87, 89n23, 93n33, 95, 99n53, 105n79, 108n85, 109, 110
Chance, J. Bradley, 83
Chanikuzhy, Jacob, 48n72, 49, 73n24, 81n46, 100n58, 106n80, 108n88, 109n92
Collins, Adela Yarbro, 1n3
Collins, Raymond F., 92
Coloe, Mary L., 101, 102n63
Congar, Yves M.-J., 46n64, 55n102,
Conzelmann, Hans, 42n49, 83n55
Cranfield, C. E. B., 31n3, 49n76, 50n82, 58n113, 59
Crossley, James G., 34
Croy, N. Clayton, 103n66, 104
Cullmann, Oscar, 85n4
Culpepper, R. Alan, 33–34, 36, 47n67, 85n4, 96n46

Danker, Frederick W., 73n27, 75n31
Davies, W. D., 1n4, 9n9, 16n36, 17n42, 19n52, 21, 22n62
Dawsey, J. M., 80n45
Derrett, J. D. M., 44n55, 48n72, 49,
Dillon, R. J., 66n9
Dodd, C. H., 92, 99, 105
Donahue, John R., 37n35, 38, 39n40, 43, 48n72
Duff, Paul B., 47, 48n72
Duling, D. C., 19n49

Edersheim, Alfred, 92, 93n31

Index of Authors

Edwards, James R., 50n81
Ellis, E. Earle, 75n30
Evans, Craig A., 11n16, 24n69, 27n78, 48n72, 49n74, 50n80, 57n109, 77

Fay, Ron C., 82nn50–51
Fee, Gordon D., 87, 88n21
Fitzmyer, Joseph A., 45n60, 65n2, 67n13, 74n29, 77, 80n44
Ford, J. M., 56n106
France, R. T., 1n4, 10n11, 10n13, 11n19, 11n20, 12, 13n26, 15n32, 15n34, 16n38, 17n40, 17n41, 19n52, 20n53, 21n59, 31n3, 38n37, 39n40, 41n46, 44n55, 48n72, 50, 52, 53n96, 56n106, 60n121, 61n122, 100n56
Fredricksen, Paula, 58n113
Fuller, R. H., 42n49

Glancy, Jennifer, 105, 106
Goulder, M. D., 9n9, 77n42
Gray, Timothy C., 46n65, 59n118
Guelich, R. A., 36
Gundry, Robert H., 1n4, 8n2, 14, 19n52, 31n3, 33, 38n36, 39, 40, 41n45, 43n53, 50n81, 54n101, 56, 59n118
Guthrie, Donald, 35n20

Haenchen, Ernst, 93, 96n45, 100n54
Hagner, D. A., 1n4, 10n10, 10n11, 10n14, 10n15, 11n16, 11n20, 12, 15, 16n35, 19n52, 22n63, 25n71
Hahn, Ferdinand, 42n49
Hall, C. A., 32n4
Harrington, Daniel J., 37n35, 38, 39n40, 43, 48n72
Hendricksen, William, 99n53
Hengel, Martin, 31n3, 85n3, 85n6
Higgins, A. J. B., 42n49
Hooker, Morna D., 45nn60–61, 48, 49n76, 50, 51, 52, 53, 57, 59
Horsley, Richard A., 8
Hummel Reinhart, 9n9
Hurtado, Larry, 48, 49n73

Juel, Donald, 58n113, 60n121

Keener, Craig S., 1n4, 31n3, 32, 86n16, 89, 93n33, 94, 100n56, 105n75
Kerr, R. Alan, 108
Kingsbury, J. D., 12
Kinman, Brent, 21n55, 73n24, 81
Koester, Craig R., 92
Köstenberger, Andreas J., 31n3, 84n2
Kümmel, W. G., 31n3

Lane, William L., 32, 37n31, 37n32, 43n53, 44n55, 45n59, 49, 50n82, 53
Liefeld, W. L., 73n27
Lightfoot, R. H., 99
Lincoln, Andrew T., 88, 97n48
Lindars, Barnabas, 100n55
Loader, W. R. G., 19n49

Maas, Anthoy, 13n27
Maddox, Robert, 67n14
Manson, T. W., 22n60, 52
Marcus, Joel, 35, 39
Marshall, I. Howard, 2n6, 66n6, 69n19, 70n21, 73n25, 77n38, 81nn47–48
Matson, M. A., 105n74
Meier, John P., 9n7
Metzger, Bruce, 12n22, 103n67
Michaels, J. Ramsey, 100n56
Milne, Bruce, 85n5
Moloney, Francis J., 107n81, 108n89
Moo, Douglas, 9n8, 32, 35, 36, 37n34, 66, 70n22
Moore, Stephen D., 4n8
Moritz, T., 33, 40n43
Morris, Leon, 93n33, 99n53
Moulton, H. K., 104
Myers, Ched, 34n16

Nereparampil, L., 107n82, 110n93
Neufeld, Thomas R., 104
Nolland, John, 8, 73n26, 82n54
Novakovic, Lidija, 43n51

Oden, Thomas C., 32n4
O'Toole, Robert F., 4
Overman, J. A., 10n12

Painter, John, 100n56

142

Index of Authors

Perkins, Perkins, 58n114
Perschbacher, W. J., 56n105
Pitts, A. W., 84n2
Porter, Stanley E., 84n2
Prins, E. J., 42n49

Qualls, P. F., 61n123

Radcliffe, Timothy, 34n16
Repschinski, Boris, 18, 19n51
Richardson, Peter, 1n3
Robbins, V. K., 66n9
Robinson, J. A. T., 65, 66, 99n52

Saldarini, Anthony J., 10n12, 57, 58n112
Sanders, E. P., 28, 58n113, 60
Schnackenburg, Rudolf, 100n59
Schnelle, Udo, 37n35, 39n40
Schröter, Jens, 33n12
Schwarz, Hans, 43n51
Sim, David C., 10n12
Smith, C. W. F., 22n60
Song, Young-mog, 68
Stein, R. H., 35, 44, 45n60, 48n72, 50n81, 56, 57n109, 75n33
Stendahl, Krister, 9n7
Strauss, Mark L., 73n23
Strecker, Georg, 9n7

Tan, Randall, 4
Tannehill, R. C., 65n3, 76
Tatum, W. Barnes, 48n72

Taylor, Vincent, 50n82
Teeple, H. M., 42n49
Telford, William R., 31n3, 52n95, 59
Theissen, Gerd, 34n16
Thiede, Carsten P., 77n39
Tödt, Heinz E., 42n49
Torrey, Charles Cutler, 34n16
Toussaint, Stanley D., 92n28
Twelftree, Graham H., 94

Unger, Merrill F., 57n110

Van Iersel, Bas M. F., 42, 43n53, 44n55, 45, 48n72, 51n87
Vistar, Deolito Jr. V., 97n47, 101n62

Walker, P. W. L., 62n125
Watts, Rikki E., 40
Weinert, F. D., 82nn52–53, 83
Wenham, John W., 34n16
Whitacre, R. A., 100n56
Willits, Joel, 4
Winn, Adam, 36
Witherington, Ben, 95, 100n56, 107n83, 108n89
Wohlgemut, J. R., 112
Wrede, William, 33–34
Wright, N. T., 27, 58n113

Yarbrough, R. W., 31n3

Zahn, Theodore B., 35n20

Index of Ancient Documents

OLD TESTAMENT/ HEBREW BIBLE

Genesis
27:28	96
50:1	77

Exodus
23:20	40
30:11–16	102n64

Leviticus
21:16–20	18

Numbers
11:13	77
19:2	73

Deuteronomy
21:3	73

Judges
11:37–38	77

1 Samuel
6:7	73
8:17	49

2 Samuel
5:8	18
6:3	73
6:6	18n46
7:12–16	16
19–20	15

1 Kings
1:33	74
33:53	26

2 Kings
8:11	77
9:13	49

Nehemiah
10:32	102n64
11:17	26

Psalms
8:3	19
8:4	20
69:9	107
113–118	44
118	45
118:25–26	44, 48
118:26	74
136:9	77

Ecclesiastes
9:7	96

Isaiah
25:6	96
28:3–4	52
40:3	40

Isaiah (continued)

56	26, 60, 80
56:1–2	60
56:3–8	61
56:7	25–26, 28, 57, 62, 80, 83
56:9–12	61
62:11	15

Jeremiah

7	80
7:11	25, 26, 27, 57, 80
8:13	52
9:2	77
13:17	77
14:7	77
52:4	77

Ezekiel

11:23	15
43:2	15

Daniel

7:13–14	42

Hosea

9:10	52
9:16	52

Joel

1:7	52
1:12	52
2:19	96
3:18	96

Amos

9:13	96

Micah

7:1	52

Zechariah

9	48, 74
9:9	14, 14n29, 15, 48–51
9:9–10	74
10:6–7	96

14:4	15, 50
14:21	106

Malachi

3:1	40, 74, 106
3:3	106

APOCRYPHA

Sir

51:14	26

Bar

1:10–14	26

2 Macc

10:26	26

3 Macc

2:10	26

PSEUDEPIGRAPHA

T. Moses

7:8–10	24

NEW TESTAMENT

Matthew

1:1–4:16	12
1:1–4:11	13
1:1–18	16n36
1:1	12
1:21	9n5, 21
1:22–23	16n36
1:22	11n20,
2:1–12	16n36
2:4	19
2:5	11n20
2:15	11n20
2:17	11n20

2:23	11n20	21:7	14n29
3:3	11n20	21:8–9	17
3:11	16n36	21:8	17
4:12–16:20	13, 68	21:9	16, 16n36
4:14	11n20	21:10–11	18, 21
4:17–16:20	12	21:10	16n36, 17, 45n63, 55
4:17	12	21:11	16n36, 17
4:23–24	18	21:12–13	1, 2, 7, 20–28
4:23	17n39	21:12	13, 20, 21, 22
5	67	21:13	20
5:17	11	21:14–17	2, 5, 7, 14, 17–20, 28
5:41	49	21:14	13, 18
7:28	12	21:18–22	51
8:1	17n39	21:18–19	80
8:16	18	23:15	25n72
8:17	11n20	23:17	109
9:35	18	23:35	109
11:1	12	23:37	41
11:3	16n36	24:2	28
11:10	11n20	25:34	12
11:13	11	26:1	12
11:29	16n36	26:20	85n8
12:15	17n39, 18	26:31	11n20
12:17	11n20	26:56	11n20
13:14–15	11n20	27:5	109
13:35	11n20	27:9	11n20
13:53	12	27:32	49
13:57	16n36	27:40	109
14:13	17n39	28:18–20	25n72
14:14	18		
15:30–31	18		
16:21–28:20	12		
16:21–20:34	13		
16:21	12, 16n36		
17:24–27	102n64		
19–20	68		
19:1	12		
19:2	17n39, 18		
19:28	12		
20:17	16n36		
20:29	16		
21:1–28:15	13		
21:1–11	2, 5, 7, 14, 16, 28		
21:1–4	14		
21:1	15, 16n36		
21:4–5	16n36		
21:4	11n20, 14, 15, 16n36		
21:5	15, 16n36		

Mark

1:1–8:26	40, 68
1:1–8:21	41
1:1	37
1:14	13
1:16–20	38
1:22	57
3:13–19	38
4:10–34	38
4:35–41	38
5:21–43	51
5:37–43	38
6:1–3	60
6:6–13	38
6:7–13	38
6:30–44	38
6:45–52	38

Index of Ancient Documents

Mark (continued)

7:1–23	38, 67
8:1–10	38
8:22–10:52	41, 43
8:27–16:8	40
8:27–10:45	38
8:31–32	42
8:31	42
8:34	39
9:2–8	38
9:11	57
10	68
10:32–34	42
10:33	42
10:46–52	46
10:47–48	51
10:47	42
10:48	42
11:1–16:8	41
11	49, 52, 61
11:1–11	5, 30, 41–51, 58, 61
11:1–10	43, 45, 50
11:1–6	43–44
11:1	47
11:2	43, 46, 49
11:3	43, 49–50
11:4–6	44
11:7	44
11:8–10	44–45
11:8	44, 49
11:9	44, 48, 50
11:10	16, 42, 44–45, 50
11:11	55
11:11–12	43
11:12	80
11:12–21	51
11:12–14	5, 14n28, 30, 51–52, 61–62, 80
11:13	52
11:15–19	1, 5, 14n28, 30, 51, 53–62
11:15–18	100
11:15–16	55–56
11:15	45, 55, 80
11:16	45, 58–59
11:17	57, 59–60
11:18	57–58
11:27	45
11:20–26	5, 30, 51–52
11:20–25	14n28
11:21–28	60
11:27–33	51, 61
11:28	58, 100
12:35	45
13	35, 36
13:1–37	38
13:1–2	36
13:2	45, 77
14:3–9	43
14:3	41
14:12–26	38
14:17	85n8
14:28	38
14:49	45
14:58	100, 109
15:21	49
15:29	100, 109
16:7	38

Luke

1:1–4	66–67
1:5–25	83
1:21	109
1:32	74
1:46–55	70
1:47	69n20
1:54–55	69
1:68–79	69
1:69	69n20
1:71	69n20
1:77	69n20
2:1	67
2:11	69n20
2:20	69n20
2:29–32	69
2:37	26
3:1–2	67
3:6	69n20
4:14–9:17	68
4:14	13
4:18–19	69
4:18	70
4:25–27	70, 76
5:27–32	70
6:20–23	70

Index of Ancient Documents

7:1–10	70	19:37	72, 75–76
7:11–17	69	19:38	16, 72, 74, 75
7:16	76	19:39–40	72
7:20	75	19:41–44	5, 64, 71, 76–78
7:22	70	19:42	77
7:28	70	19:45–46	1, 5, 13n28, 64, 79–82, 83
7:30	70	19:46	81, 83
7:34	70	19:47–48	5, 13n28, 71, 78
7:36–50	70	19:47	82, 83
8:1–3	70	21:1–4	70
8:16	56	21:6	77
8:48	70	22:14	85n8
9:51–19:27	68	23:34	69
10:21–22	70	24:1–12	70
10:25–37	68	24:44	69
10:30–37	70		
10:38–42	70		

John

11:11–27	73
11:16	80
11:17	80
13:10–17	70
13:13	76
13:34–35	77
13:34	41
14:13	70
14:21–24	70
15:1–2	70
15:11–32	69
16:1–9	69
16:19–31	70
17:15	76
17:18	76
18:10	26
18:35–43	73n23
18:38–39	74
18:43	76
19:1–10	69
19:7	70
19:9	69n20
19:10	69
19:11–27	73n23
19:28–40	5, 64, 71–76
19:28–44	13n28
19:28	73
19:30	43
19:32	72
19:33	73
19:35	72

1:1–18	89
1:1–2	102–103
1:1	89
1:12	108
1:14	102–103
1:18	89, 102–103
1:19–20:31	89
1:29	102–103
1:36	102–103
1:45	102
1:49	102
2:1–4:54	91
2:1–11	6, 14n28, 84, 91–96
2:1	91
2:3	93, 94, 95
2:4	93, 94, 95
2:5	95
2:6	95
2:7	95
2:11	91, 92, 108
2:13–22	1, 14n28, 84, 98–110
2:13	101
2:14–15	104–105, 109
2:14	102, 103
2:15–16	103–108
2:15	80, 102, 104
2:16	105, 109
2:18–22	108–110
2:18	100, 108
2:19	100, 108–111

Index of Ancient Documents

John *(continued)*

2:20	109–110
2:21	109–111
2:22	109
2:23–25	6, 84, 96–97
2:23	108
3:16	108
3:18	108
4:21	93
4:45	13
4:46	91
4:48	108
5:17	108
5:28–29	94
6:26	108
6:30	108
7:13	93
7:30	93, 94
8:20	94
9:22	88
10:41	108
11:35	77
11:55	13
12:13	16
12:23	94
12:27	94
12:37	108
12:42	88
13–16	86
13:1	94
13:23–24	86n9
13:23	85
16:2	88
17:1	94
17:5	89
18:31–33	86
18:37–38	86
20:2–9	86n9
20:13	93
20:30–31	87–88, 91, 97, 108
20:31	87
21:1–25	89
21:2	86
21:20	86n9

Acts

2:12	32
2:17	109
2:22–24	40
2:25	32
2:36	40
7:48	109
11:19–30	65
13:1–3	65
13:5	32
13:13	32
15:30–35	65
15:37	32
16:10–17	65
20:5–15	65
21:1–18	65
27:1–28:16	65

Romans

8:4	12n21
9:12	56
12:5	110
16:13	36

1 Corinthians

3:16	109
3:17	109
12:12	110

2 Corinthians

5:17	92
6:16	109

Ephesians

2:21	109

Colossians

4:10	32

Philemon

24	32

2 Timothy

4:11	32

1 Peter

5:13	32, 36

Index of Ancient Documents

Revelation
5:6	109
5:8	109
14:15	109
16:1	109
16:17	109

DEAD SEA SCROLLS

1QS
2.5–22	18

1QM
7.5–6	18n48

CD
15.15–17	18n48

PHILO

Spec. Laws
1.78	102

JOSEPHUS

Vita
189–96	24

C. Ap.
2.196	26

A.J.
3.194–196	102
3.230	23
17.213–218	81

B.J.
7.218	102
11.332–36	47

RABBINIC WRITINGS

m. Ker.
1.7	24n67
6.8	23

b. Pesaḥ.
57a	24, 27

m. Sukkah
1.1	56
1.3	56
1.6	56

Ber.
9.5	56, 59n117, 103

t. Ketub.
13.3	102n65

m. Bek.
8.7	102n65

Tg. Jer.
7.9	27
7.11	27
8.10	27
23.11	27

GRECO-ROMAN WRITINGS

Plutarch
Ant.
24.3–4	47

Index of Ancient Documents

EARLY CHRISTIAN WRITINGS

1 Clement
5	34

Eusebius
Hist. eccl.
3.39.15	31, 34–35
3.4.2	65
6.14.5–7	32, 35–36
6.25.5	32, 35

Justin Martyr
Dial.
103.19	65
106	31
106.3	35

Irenaeus
Haer.
3.1.1	34
3.1.2	31, 36
3.14.1	65

Tertullian
Marc.
4.5	32

www.ingramcontent.com/pod-product-compliance
Lightning Source LLC
Chambersburg PA
CBHW071505150426
43191CB00009B/1425